Ramanachala

Impact of Sri Ramana Maharshi

2021.1231

Srinivas Shastri

Shri SiddhGanesh Mandir, Gwarighat, Jabalpur

Cover Photo taken in: **Sri Ramanasramam, Tiruvannamalai**
Cover Photo by: **Author**
Author Photo by: **NSS Prakasa Sastry**

Hardcover ISBN: 9798758024546
Paperback ISBN: 9798479466304

To Balan

Who led me to Arunachala

To Michelle, one of a kind...ness

Who made me fearless on the eve of my Aortic Valve operation in May 2013, with a "reading" from Ramanachala

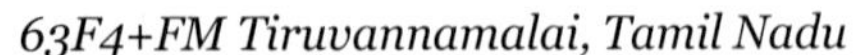

63F4+FM Tiruvannamalai, Tamil Nadu

Sri Ramanasramam

In Gratitude

With heartfelt thanks to:

- Balan, for his meticulous reviews of chapters as they were being added
- Michelle, whose copious continual feedback spurred me on to finish the book
- Ajoy and Sivaram, for their energizing comments
- PSM, for letting me use his "3D" experience
- HPR, Balan, Gopa, Bob, and Macha, for the trips to Arunachala
- David Godman, for letting me use excerpts from his books
- Arunachala, who i was facing all the while from my study, looking southeast from Bengaluru, while working on the book on my 22" LG Chromebase

None of us is as good as all of us
~Ray Kroc

Notes

- **Bhagavan** refers to Ramanachala
  - **The Power of Arunachala** is a famous article written by Michael James and hosted on davidgodman.org
- **Master** refers to Sri Ramakrishna
  - **Gospel** refers to the book **The Gospel of Sri Ramakrishna**
- **Swami** refers to Sri Satya Sai Baba of "Put-apart-the-i"
- **Boldfacing** in quotes used is by the author, unless otherwise specified
- This document uses US spellings and follows the Times of India Edit Page style of using the lower-case **i**, except at the start of sentences. The Big I refers to the Self, in which all things appear and disappear
- All photos/images are shot/made by the author, unless otherwise indicated
- The caption for photos will indicate the **place** where it was taken, as far as possible. Where feasible, the **Plus Codes** for the place will be indicated *right-justified* at the top of the photo. You can enter the Plus Codes in the Search box of gMaps [Google Maps] to **directly** visit that place
- Numbo Jumbo means Numerology, which i do for fun
- The plural of *Indian words* will be the same word; suffixing them with an **s** seems to be a travesty
- Feel that the period is superfluous at the end of paragraphs

Table of Contents

ARUNACHALA
GOODS
TN24
U6388
CARRIER

Introduction

On Wednesday 25th Aug 2021, realized that the 125th anniversary of a boy coming to Arunachala in Tiruvannamalai and staying put was coming up the following Wednesday [1st Sept 2021]

In 1896, a 16-year-old boy called Venkataraman was pulled by some mysterious force to Arunachala and became *achala* [stationary] for the remaining 54 years, till 1950

This book is about the impact that Ramanachala [*ramaṇāchala*] has had and continues to have on me through dreams, experiences, and ideas, to be at ease with an exploding/imploding world

More importantly, i don't have to change the world, **it's enough if i changed myself and the world would change to that extent**. As Ramanachala said:

> Wanting to reform the world without discovering one's true self is like trying to cover the world with leather to avoid the pain of walking on stones and thorns. It is much simpler to wear shoes

As it is, the world is an **appearance** in the Self and is a reflection and resound of one's karma, thoughts, words, and deeds

The life of Ramanachala has been well documented and will **not** be the subject of this book

Enough material exists on the Net such as:

https://en.wikipedia.org/wiki/Ramana_Maharshi

The reader can also refer to some of the following books, which have been my inspiration for long

https://flic.kr/p/8UGJrk

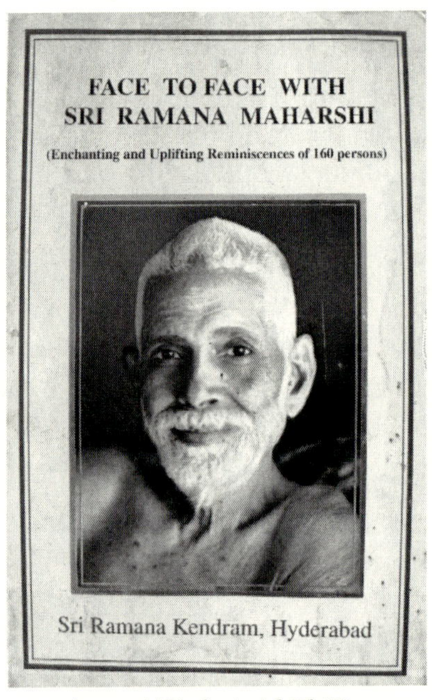

https://flic.kr/p/7hXbT8

RAMANA PERIYA PURANAM

(Inner Journey of 77 Old Devotees)

V.Ganesan

https://flic.kr/p/eRaEpc

https://flic.kr/p/9AUi29

This book will be the **intersection** of material on Ramanachala and how He affected me through dreams, experiences, and ideas, in more or less a chronological order

Someone asked Ramanachala to summarize His teaching in **one** *word. He said:* ***Attention***

Knowledge isn't free. You have to pay attention
~Richard Feynman

Row, row, row your boat
Gently down the stream
Merrily merrily, merrily, merrily
Life is but a dream

An Incarnation by Death

What defines an Incarnation?

There was an event in May 2002 when I had an interesting realization of God being **within**

Two observations as a prelude to the same:

- Edgar Cayce, my first guru, says that the soul enters the body at the time of delivery, **not** at the time of conception. From a karmic design standpoint, this makes a lot of sense (based on the condition of the body, allocate the soul). So, naturally, one person wondered who/what sustains the fetus. Edgar Cayce answered that it was the Spirit
- The Mandukya Upanishad talks of two birds on the branch of a tree. One is going through the pleasure and pain of Life, while the other is just a Witness

A while later, i hired a driver for my car. One day, while driving back home with him, i observed the following:

- All along, i was driving
- When the driver came in, i moved to the background

It struck me that it's the same at the time of a baby's delivery. The Spirit moves to the background and is an observer for the rest of one's Life

In the case of Incarnations, there's no soul allocated at the time of delivery. The Spirit that sustained the fetus through its nine months continues as the driver for the rest of the Incarnation's life

To all those who wonder why an Incarnation has to suffer like ordinary mortals, the Master observes:

> "Even a judge, while giving evidence in a case, comes down and stands in the witness-box"

This is what i call the **Driver~GoD** [Guardian of Driver :-)] metaphor and we can use it to explain the *jīva* [a mortal] and various types of incarnations

A Mortal [*jīva*]

Conception: The fetus starts developing, sustained by the Spirit (GoD)

Delivery: The soul is allocated and GoD goes to the background (does back-seat driving from then on, as the Conscience)

Death: Soul exits body, along with GoD

Incarnation by Birth

Conception: The fetus starts developing, sustained by the Spirit (GoD), as usual. Mother might have visions of gods and angels

Delivery: No soul is allocated at the time of delivery. The Spirit that sustained the fetus through its nine months continues as the driver for the rest of the incarnation's life. Due to this, His actions are spontaneous and rarely, if ever, out of sync with *dharma*. Seen in the case of Jesus Christ and Sri Ramakrishna

Death: Normally referred to as *samādhi*; GoD exits body

Incarnation by Death

The interesting thing is that this metaphor holds good even in the case of incarnations by death such as Ramanachala

In His own words: (**Face to Face with Sri Ramana Maharshi**, page 2)

> About six weeks before I left Madurai for good, a great change took place in my life. It was quite sudden. I was sitting alone in a room in my uncle's house, when a sudden fear of death overtook me. There was nothing in my state of health to account for it. I just felt, "I am going to die" and began thinking about it. The fear of death drove my mind inwards and I said to myself mentally, "Now that death has come; what does it mean? What is it that is dying? Only this body dies". And at once I dramatized the occurrence of death. I held my breath and kept my lips tightly closed and said to myself, "This body is dead. It will be carried to the cremation ground and reduced to ashes. But with the death of this body am I dead? Is this body 'I'? I am the spirit transcending the body. That means I am the deathless atman"

As i see it, at the point of death of the *jīva* called Venkatraman, due to some inexplicable reason, GoD didn't exit the body along with the driver. He just took over the driver's place and drove the body for 54 more years. That's why i call Ramanachala an incarnation by death, a unique instance in recorded times

Girivalam with Balan ~ 2007

Day 1: Saturday 14th April 2007

Had been planning this trip for a while, so it was nice to be actually able to do it

Picked up Balan at the CSB Junction in Bengaluru and soon we were at the Om Shakthi Maha Ganapathi temple. Had a couple of unusual experiences here, so always make it a point to say hello to the Fat Man and the Old Mother, who was looking gorgeous, here

Had burned 10 CDs from the **Sundaram Sai Bhajan** cornucopia and Balan was quite appreciative of them and kept increasing the volume. It was a good thing as my voice had totally gone due to the cold and cough earlier on in the week

The National Highway, NH7, was a beautiful black ribbon once we got past Hosur and it was a terrific pleasure to drive on something like that

Soon we were at the Reliance A-1 Plaza, where we knocked off some much-needed *idli* and coffee. The doors on the loo were amusing: like those on Western saloons

At the half-way point, Krishnagiri, we had to peel off this lovely NH and get back on to the State Highway, a dangerous proposition as the SHs don't have medians. Anyway, as Balan said, it was so much greener and more enjoyable, if you could address the occasional pothole and veer away from the oncoming traffic

The bhajans were really good at this stage and Balan was wondering what happens during the bhajans. Guess he was surprised by the "non-denominational" aspects of it (all the Hindu gods and then some others are covered in some really stirring soulful stuff)

7M57+5Q Anandhavadi, Tamil Nadu

We suddenly pulled up for this unusual sight: a vermilion-covered termite mound

Some of the imagery in India leaves me stunned

Soon we were in the vicinity of Tiruvannamalai, and we were discussing the recent articles of Deepak Chopra in ToI where he was writing stuff similar to what Peter Russell raised in his article on **Reality & Consciousness**. Even though i accept the fact that everything happens in the mind, it doesn't really explain how everyone else is experiencing a similar material world. I concluded that the best explanation would be that the Universe is a dream of God, in which we are **all** participants. Better a top-down approach than a bottom-up one, in this case

It was around 1:15 PM when we reached Sri Ramanasramam and stopped for lunch at an ashram, slightly further ahead. The *thāli* was delicious and cost just ₹19 each. Across our table, a person with a pleasant face was seated, so i struck up a conversation with him. He had just finished his visit to the ashram and had seen the Arunachaleswara Temple in the morning. He was an accountant at a granite firm in Chittoor and was happy with his work

We made our way to the SRMOAH [Sri Ramana Maharshi Old Age Home], where Balan has a room that he uses as a spiritual retreat. This is a lovely place and i had the good fortune of staying here in an earlier visit in 2003, along with HPRamesh, my Infosys pal

62FW+CP Tiruvannamalai, Tamil Nadu

Arunachala from **Sri Ramana Maharshi Old Age Home**

The view of Arunachala from here is always uplifting and reminds me of Mt. 11:28:

> *Come to Me, all you who labor and are heavy laden, and I will give you rest*

The garden had many trees, drooping with many mangoes, more than you can eat!

After some rest, we made our way to Sri Ramanasramam in the evening. The Saturday *pārāyaṇa* was nice and i particularly liked the song that went:

> *Ramana Sadguru, Ramana Sadguru*
> *Ramana Sadguru, Rāyané*

We had a quick dinner of *chapāthi* and *uthappam*. On the way out, we met Johnny, from LA, who was enjoying his tryst with the Self and bemoaning the fact that India, which had such natural people, was aping the West

Since it was the day (14th April) that Ramanachala attained *samādhi*, there was a rendition of the song that he was listening to when that happened. We went back for that and it was one on Arunachala Siva. It was a Tamil song that one could easily chip in on the refrain. Noticed that Arunachala was one more in the small list of famous 28s [Coca-Cola, Google, Infosys] in Numbo Jumbo

Call the three of them [Arunachala, Infosys, and Google] my insurance: AIG ;-)

63F4+FM Tiruvannamalai, Tamil Nadu

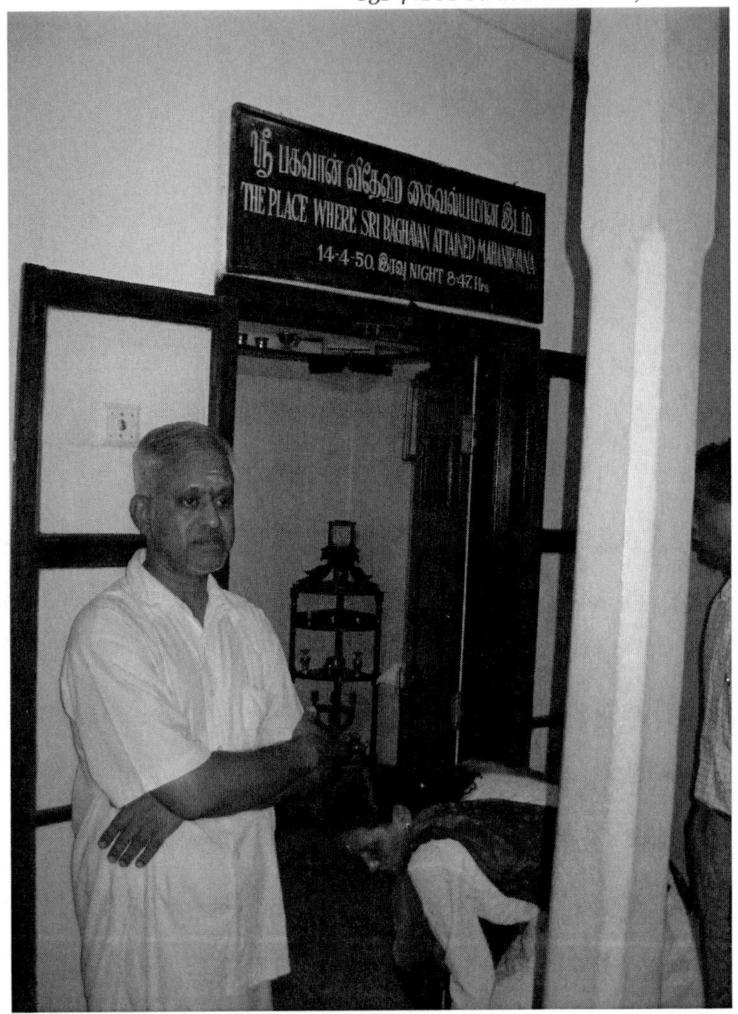

Samādhi Room at **Sri Ramanasramam**

Balan was mentioning an unusual incident pertaining to the Ganesh in the temple dedicated to the mother of Ramanachala

Read it later on in the night in the words of Lakshmana Swamy: (**Power of the Presence**, **Part Two**, page 225, top)

> By April 1950 it was clear to everyone that Bhagavan was about to give up his body. The cancer had debilitated him to such an extent, he could barely move. About a week before his death I was walking around the Mother's Temple, the one which was being consecrated on my first visit to the ashram. On my way round I stopped to look at a statue of Ganesh that had been recently garlanded. As I gazed at the statue, it began to move in its niche. The head and shoulders started to rock backwards and forwards, and each time it rocked forwards, the bowed head of Ganesh moved nearer and nearer to mine. I suddenly realized that if I stayed there any longer, the garland would slip from the statue's neck onto my own. I didn't want to be garlanded in this way, so I moved away from the statue and continued my walk around the temple

Day 2: Sunday 15th April 2007

Got up early and took a few shots of Arunachala, with wisps of cloud floating past It

62FW+CP Tiruvannamalai, Tamil Nadu

Arunachala one early morning from **SRMOAH**

Ms. VaraLakshmi, the lady who built Sri Ramana Maharshi Old Age Home, did a tremendous job of the SRMOAH. There's a huge well coupled with a tank for rainwater harvesting

Further to their right, there's a nice Lalitha temple with an unobstructed view of Arunachala

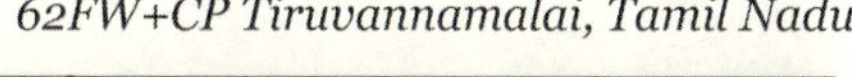
62FW+CP Tiruvannamalai, Tamil Nadu

The deity was most charming and i have always been a fan of Arunachala ;-)

Soon we set off, not to the ashram, but to Arunachala Hrudayam, the house of Lakshmana Swamy, who experienced the Self very soon after meeting Ramanachala

6393+Q7G, Tiruvannamalai, Tamil Nadu

There was only one visitor at Arunachala Hrudayam as it was a Sunday (no *darshan*). But it was most peaceful and we hung around for an hour, watching the crows sharpen their beaks on the branches of the mango trees and the peacocks crying out

Then, we got back to Sri Ramanasramam, where i was rewarded with this peacock on a hoarding of Ramanachala, especially the way the tail "washed" across the forehead

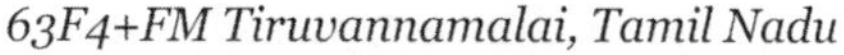
63F4+FM Tiruvannamalai, Tamil Nadu

There's a *nārāyaṇa seva* at 11 AM, before the lunch at the ashram at 11:30 AM. Nice to see that folks get some excellent food at least once a day

We had brunch and retired to SRMOAH. Lay supine reading the starting chapter by Kunju Swami in **The Power of the Presence, Part Two**. On page 25 (top), one reads about the two verses that Bhagavan copied from the Sanskrit version of the **Arunachala Mahatmyam**:

> What cannot be acquired without endless pains—the true import of Vedanta—is easily attained by all those who can directly sight this hill or even mentally think of it from afar
>
> I [Siva] ordain that residence within three *yōjana* [a *yōjana* is about 12~15 km] of this hill shall by itself suffice to burn off all defects and effect union with the Supreme, even in the absence of initiation

Was thinking of taking it easy while Balan did the *girivalam* [*pradakshina* or going around Arunachala] in the afternoon. However, Ramanachala was extolling it no end in the same chapter by Kunju Swami: (pp. 55~56)

> Sri Bhagavan always spoke highly of *pradakshina* and encouraged many devotees to go as often as possible. The following story shows just how highly he regarded the practice. A Tiruvannamalai sadhu used to go round the hill every day, without fail, but other than that he did not do any meditation, japa or other practice. One day he asked Sri Bhagavan for a particular book, so Sri Bhagavan asked me to get it and give it to him. Later Sri Bhagavan asked me whether I had handed over the book
>
> I told him that I had and then asked Sri Bhagavan, 'That sadhu is not doing anything other than *pradakshina*. He does not seem to know about anything else. What does he want this book for?'
>
> Sri Bhagavan replied, 'What is there superior to *pradakshina*? That alone is sufficient. Even if you sit and do *japa*, the mind will wander, but if you do *pradakshina* the mind will remain one-pointed even though the limbs and the body are moving. Doing *japa* or meditation with a one-pointed mind, while moving about, without having any thought other than the *japa*, is known as *sanchāra samādhi* [absorption while moving]. That is why in the olden days pilgrimage on foot, without using any other conveyance, had so much importance

'*Giri pradakshina* is unique. As there are many types of herbs on the hill, the breeze that blows over them is good for the body. Even today there are many *siddha* and great souls on the hill. They too go around the hill, but we cannot see them. Because of this, when we do *pradakshina* we should keep to the **left** of the road. If we do this, we do *pradakshina* without causing any inconvenience to them. We also get the merit of walking round these great souls, thereby receiving their blessings. As we do *pradakshina*, the body becomes healthy and the mind attains the peace of the Self. Because of all these things, *pradakshina* is an extraordinary sadhana'

In the course of his talk Sri Bhagavan also mentioned many other points that emphasised the greatness of *pradakshina*. I was extremely happy to hear from Sri Bhagavan himself about the greatness of *pradakshina*. From then on I felt enthusiastic about *pradakshina*, and the thought of going always filled me with joy

So i quickly joined Balan and set out. He wanted to keep silent on the *girivalam*, so i moved on and quickly completed the *pradakshina* of about 14 km in three hours flat (4~7 PM), resting only for about two minutes at 5:15 PM

722Q+QX Adi Annamalai, Tamil Nadu

Arunachala from **Adi Annamalai Temple**

During the *girivalam*, captured many moods of Arunachala

There were some nice views, though none to beat the one at SRMOAH, IMHO

Day 3: Monday 16th April 2007

With the help of one of the inmates at Sri Ramanasramam, Balan had organized an early-morning *abhishekam* at Arunachaleswara Temple, the humongous temple at the base of Arunachala. Since it was a Monday, the day of Siva, i accepted the invite with alacrity

We were at the ashram by 6 AM, where we were rewarded with this peacock in silhouette. They are a big hit with the little kids and keep them engrossed with their raucous cries

63F4+FM Tiruvannamalai, Tamil Nadu

Peacock at **Sri Ramanasramam**

Then we "auto"ed to the Arunachaleswara Temple by 6:30 AM. When we got into the inner courtyard, found a huge pink Ganesha to the left of the main temple, which startled me no end

The main *abhishēkam* started at 7:30 AM and it was a visual treat. All the decorations on the *lingam* were removed and the bare stone worshiped with milk, honey, etc. Universal foam!

It reminded me of this observation by the Master in the **Gospel**: (Chapter **31. Advice to Ishan**)

> When do I call Him Brahman? When He is inactive and unattached to work. A man may put on clothes, yet he remains the same man as when he was naked. He was naked, now he is clothed. He may again take off his clothes

The abiding memory from this was the appearance of an outline of the **Third Eye** on the *lingam* after each of the Universal Foam elements was washed away with water!

The main priest was a dour character, but there were two other priests that i really liked. One of them was handing over the stuff to worship in a jiffy; breaking open a jar of honey with its tight lid, emptying a 50-litre can of milk into manageable chunks, opening/closing the curtain in a trice, etc. Man, he was really fast; his body was glistening with sweat with all the exertion in a cramped space with so many folks, but there was a constant smile on his face. A real inspiration!

Folks were moving up and down the room, but everyone would adjust. I was right in the middle of that movement; huge vessels would swing within inches of my face, but it was all good fun. All during the *abhishēkam* was a constant chant of Tamil songs, which really got into my system even though i couldn't understand what they meant

This was followed by the *abhishēkam* at the Old Mother's temple, which moved me even more

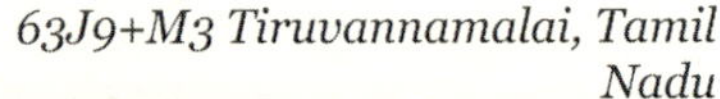
63J9+M3 Tiruvannamalai, Tamil Nadu

Skandashram from
Arunachaleswara Temple

Then we got out into the outer courtyard where Balan pointed me to Skandashram, which was Ramanachala's original ashram right on Arunachala, before He moved to Sri Ramanasramam soon after His mother's death in May 1922

You can ID Skandashram by the grove of trees in the pic

Then we ran into this elephant

63J9+M3 Tiruvannamalai, Tamil Nadu

Elephant at **Arunachaleswara Temple**

All wonderful things must come to an end and we were soon winging our way back to Bengaluru. With so much happening over two days, both of us were quiet on the way back, listening to the lovely Sundaram Sai bhajans

63F4+FM Tiruvannamalai, Tamil Nadu

What Brahmacharya really means

Celibacy isn't hereditary

One thing i really love about the Sadguru is how well they cut right to the bone with the minimum of fuss. You get the message without the mess!

If you can't explain it simply, you don't understand it well enough~Albert Einstein

A person has converted from one religion to another. When he visits Sai Baba of Shirdi, the Saint slaps him and says: "You've changed your father!"

Ramanachala succinctly says:

> The guru provides the *guri* [aim]

Vishwanath Swami, one of His disciples whom i really admire, writes: (**The Power of the Presence**, **Part Two**, pp. 233~234)

> "Bhagavan", I asked, "how am I to rise above my present animal existence? My own efforts in that direction have proved futile and I am convinced that only a superior power can transform me. That is what has brought me here"

> Bhagavan replied with great compassion: "Yes, you are right. It is only by awakening a power mightier than the senses and the mind that these can be subdued. If you awaken and nurture the growth of that power within you, everything else will be conquered. One should sustain the current of meditation uninterruptedly. Moderation in food and similar restraints will be helpful in maintaining the inner poise"
>
> It was the gracious advice of Bhagavan that gave a new direction to my spiritual career. A new faith was kindled within me and I found in Bhagavan the strength and support to guide me forever
>
> On another day, when I questioned him about the problem of *brahmacharya*, Bhagavan replied: "To live and move in Brahman is real *brahmacharya*. Continence, of course, is very helpful and indispensable to achieve that end. But so long as you identify yourself with the body, you can never escape sex-thoughts and distractions. It is only when you realize that you are formless pure awareness that gender-distinction disappears for good. That is *brahmacharya*, effortless and spontaneous"

Sri Brahmachaitanya Maharaj, an incarnation of Hanuman, had the firm belief that *nāma* could do what Ramanachala was referring to. His *pravachan* [discourses], just a page a day, talk about the power of *nāma* from various angles

Rid of my seed,
Cleansed of my mind
~Unknown

Later, was quite surprised to read this frank and funny stuff by Annamalai Swami in **Face to Face with Sri Ramana Maharshi**: (Section 70)

> I had hired both men and women for the construction of the dining hall. Some of the women were quite attractive and I was occasionally troubled by sexual desires. I told Bhagavan, "I don't want *mōksha*, I just want that the desire for women should not enter my mind". Bhagavan laughed and said, "**All the mahatmas are striving only for this**" To avoid sexual thoughts, I decided to do away with women workers. Bhagavan did not approve of this. He saw no reason why the women should lose their jobs merely because I was unable to control my mind

Forget about ordinary mortals, even Rakhal, later Swami Brahmananda, struggled with it. To help him out of that, the Master wrote a mantra on his tongue. In **How to Live with God**, the Master says that the mantra devours lust (page 103)

Swami Vivekananda makes a wonderful point. In **Life of Swami Brahmananda**, we read the Swami saying:

> "Many people mistakenly imagine that it is enough if one avoids the company of women, but Naren expressed the truth beautifully last night. He said: 'Woman exists for

man as long as he has lust. When you are free from lust you do not see any difference between the sexes'"

In the **Shri Sai Satcharita**, Shirdi Sai Baba advises Nanasaheb Chandorkar, who's agitated on seeing the rare beauty of a Muslim lady who had come for Baba's darshan: (end of chapter 49)

> "Nana, why are you getting agitated in vain? Let the senses do their allotted work, or duty, we should not meddle with their work. God has created this beautiful world and it is our duty to appreciate its beauty. The mind will get steady and calm slowly and gradually. When the front door was open, why go by the back one? When the heart is pure, there is no difficulty, whatsoever. Why should one be afraid of any one if there be no evil thought in us? The eyes may do their work, why should you feel shy and tottering?"

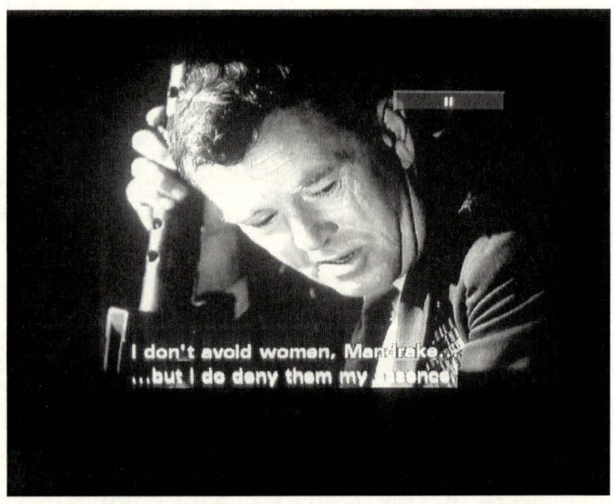

The Essence of it all ~ **Dr. Strangelove**

My Own Private Arunachala

Early May 2007, my right eye had an **arterial occlusion**, resulting in a blind spot. Thankfully, it ended up **below the fovea**, and wasn't such a debilitating one

As Swami so nicely said: (in **Sai Inspires**, 2007 May 24)

> The devotee filled with love of the Lord welcomes what may appear as punishing, as something for his good. Even when the Lord appears to be angry, His compassion is evident. Even in punishment, God's kindness will be seen

During the detailed examination at Nethradhama, Bengaluru, i noticed that it was in the shape of a B2 bomber taking off vertically. As long as it retained that shape, i thought, the blind spot was OK

Later, i felt that, to hell with the B2 bomber, it was in the shape of Arunachala!

You lose some, you win some

https://www.davidgodman.org/isanya-jnana-desikar/

After that, for more than a year, i never had migraines, with their irritating shimmering!

The doc at Nethradhama asked me to forget about the blind spot and go about my life as if nothing had happened. He was right; i got accustomed to it and noticed a very unusual benefit:

My migraines stopped completely

Earlier they would bother me at least once a month and i didn't have a single one in an entire year. As they say in software, a bug that turned out to be a feature ;-)

My migraines would start off with a visual disturbance, just below the fovea. With that area of the retina literally burnt off, there was no starting point for the migraine!

You having one of them "mindgraines"? ~ **Analyze This**

The Devotee and the Devourer

Saw an unusual line in a blog:

> Let me, Thy prey, Surrender unto Thee and be consumed, and so have peace, O Arunachala!

Saw the entire line in *aksharamanamālai* [The Marital Garland of Letters]:

> **28.** Let me, Thy prey, surrender unto Thee and be consumed, and so have Peace, Oh Arunachala!
> I came to feed on Thee, but Thou has fed on me; now there is Peace, Oh Arunachala!

God as the Devourer! Shucks, what a thought. As it is, Arunachala is the *jnānāgni* [Fire of Knowledge]

An instance in the life of the Master: (**How to Live with God**, page 37)

> Suresh Chandra Datta recorded: "Once during the *dōl* festival of Krishna, the Master went to the Radha-Krishna temple of Dakshineswar. He was then in the mood of Radha. He began to playfully spray colored powder on the image of Krishna and sang: 'While fighting today with colour, let me see whether you win or I win.' Those who witnessed the sight were overwhelmed"

The Power of Arunachala has a similar idea:

> I have seen a wonder, a magnetic hill that forcibly attracts the soul. Arresting the activities of the soul who thinks of it even once, drawing it to face itself, the One, making it thus motionless like itself, it feeds upon that sweet [pure and ripened] soul. What a wonder is this! O souls, be saved by thinking of this great Arunagiri, which shines in the mind as the destroyer of the soul [the ego]

ARUNACHALESWARAR TEMPLE, TIRUVANNAMALAI.

https://tamilnadu.dotindia.com/corporateinfo/magazine/2001jannews/Image8.jpg

The Power of Rāma nāma

Was quite touched to read this:

> Rāma Sastri from Guntur District composed eight *slōka* on Sri Bhagavan and read them out with feeling
>
> The Sastri then prayed for guidance: I am a *samsāri* unfit for *jnāna mārga*. The affairs of the world are distracting me. Please instruct me what I should do
>
> Bhagavan: Think of Bhagavan. How will the affairs of the world distract Him? You and they are in Him
>
> Devotee: May I do *nāma smarana*? What nama shall I take?
>
> Bhagavan: You are Rāma Sastri. Make that name significant. Be one with Rāma

My maternal grandpa had the same name and he was also from a place near Guntur!

Old-timers will recall the hullabaloo over the reentry of SkyLab into the Earth's atmosphere in July 1979. I think it was scheduled for reentry on July 9th, though it actually happened a couple of days later

My grandma was in her place near Guntur and joked with her friends that it would fall on them. She died the next day, on Guru *pūrnima*, Monday 9th July 1979. I can still see Mom crying in a chair at the end of the hall, when we got back from play that evening

My grandma was some lady. She used to test for her blood-sugar levels with a very involved process. Heat a test-tube along with some solution, put the drops of blood in it, and do some sort of litmus test. Can't imagine doing any of that now; the mind balks at a 5-second test! Anyway, she was one tough cookie

Some years later, my Mom told me a very unusual thing. When my grandpa died in the early 1960s, **my grandma saw a celestial chariot waiting outside the house**

The whole of one's life is the preparation for one's death

My grandpa performed a *yajna* in the 1950s. There are quite a few who say that the general well-being of his descendants is due to his austerities

What can one say, except that i was named after him?

Rooting out the ego

At the start of December 2007, i was hanging out with my kid and wondering about the size of the Universe. It's so monstrous (a billion light-years is about 10^{22} km and the Universe is at least 156 times that size) that the mind boggles

Ramanachala however dismisses this by saying that the Universe is huge only due to the vastness of the mind. He's putting it back squarely on the "seer" and, in a way, answering Bishop Berkeley's conundrum: "If a tree falls in a forest and no one's around, is there a sound?"

However, His advocated self-inquiry appears so difficult that one can't even get to first base

But there was a nice explanation by David Godman: (**An Introduction to Sri Ramana's Life and Teachings**)

> Bhagavan had a very appropriate analogy for this process. Imagine that you have a bull, and that you keep it in a stable. If you leave the door open, the bull will wander out, looking for food. It may find food, but a lot of the time it will get into trouble by grazing in cultivated fields. The owners of these fields will beat it with sticks and throw stones at it to chase it away, but it will come back again and again, and suffer repeatedly, because it doesn't understand the notion of **field boundaries**. It is just programmed to

look for food and to eat it wherever it finds something edible

The bull is the mind, the stable is the Heart where it arises and to where it returns, and the grazing in the fields represents the mind's painful addiction to seeking pleasure in outside objects. Bhagavan said that most mind-control techniques forcibly restrain the bull to stop it moving around, but they don't do anything about the bull's fundamental desire to wander and get itself into trouble. You can tie up the mind temporarily with *japa* or breath control, but when these restraints are loosened, the mind just wanders off again, gets involved in more mischief and suffers again. You can tie up a bull, but it won't like it. You will just end up with an angry, cantankerous bull that will probably be looking for a chance to commit some act of violence on you

Bhagavan likened self-enquiry to holding a bunch of fresh grass under the bull's nose. As the bull approaches it, you move away in the direction of the stable door and the bull follows you. You lead it back into the stable, and it voluntarily follows you because it wants the pleasure of eating the grass that you are holding in front of it. Once it is inside the stable, you allow it to eat the abundant grass that is always stored there. The door of the stable is always left open, and the bull is free to leave and roam about at any time. There is no punishment or restraint. The bull will go out repeatedly, because it is the nature of such animals to wander in search of food. And each time they go out, they will be punished for straying into forbidden areas. Every time you notice that your bull has wandered out, tempt it back into its stable with the same technique. Don't try to beat it into submission, or you may be attacked yourself, and don't try to solve the problem forcibly by locking it up. Sooner or later even the dimmest of bulls will understand that, since there is a perpetual supply of tasty food in the stable, there is no point wandering around outside, because that always leads to sufferings and punishments. Even though the stable door is always open, the bull will eventually stay inside and enjoy the food that is always there. This is **self-enquiry**. Whenever you find the mind wandering around in external objects and sense perceptions, take it back to its stable, which is the Heart, the source from which it rises and to which it returns. In that place it can enjoy the peace and bliss of the Self. When it wanders around outside, looking for pleasure and happiness, it just gets into trouble, but when it stays at home in the Heart, it enjoys peace and silence. Eventually, even though the stable door is always open, the mind will choose to stay at home and not wander about. Bhagavan said that the way of restraint was the way of the yogi. Yogis try to achieve restraint by forcing the mind to be still. Self-enquiry gives the mind the option of wandering wherever it wants to, and it achieves its success by gently persuading the mind that it will always be happier staying at home

In **A Heart Poured Out** by Sister Gargi, Swami Ashokananda has a very unusual XP where he almost **traps** the ego: (page 21, middle)

> One day while walking slowly to school, I felt that I had cornered my ego in one part of my body. I tried to get hold of it and throw it out. It was like a living thing. It went with lightning speed from one part of my body to the other, and with lightning speed I pursued it. I couldn't catch it. And then suddenly it became dispersed again through my whole body; it was no longer a separate thing that I could put my finger on. I have never read in the books of an experience like that, but it was very definite, very real
>
> "That was a very illuminating experience", Swami Ashokananda once said years later, attributing the experience to a friend of his, "and one which accords with our whole system of Vedantic thought. It not only gave him the sense that the ego was something different from himself; it also gave him a sense of what he really was-not the ego, but the Self.... Once you have grasped this truth, once you have brought about a little of the severance between the 'I am' and the predicate, the rest will come easily. It is as though you made a breach in a tremendous dam; it is just a matter of time before the waters themselves will sweep the whole dam away"

Dreaming of Ramanachala

From early December 2007

Was moving slightly above the ground (in an airplane?) when i saw a nice temple for Arunachala. Was thinking: "What the heck is this?", when the temple was followed by more temples and open *maṇḍapa*, in the middle of a long avenue

Was hoping to see Ramanachala when i saw Him seated in one of the *maṇḍapa*, in the same posture as in Sri Ramanasramam

Strangely enough, in another *maṇḍapa*, saw Him lying flat, face down

In both cases, He was looking towards the temple at the head of the avenue

In the dream itself, i started crying ecstatically, standing on a wall at the end of the avenue

A devotee once asked Bhagavan: "Who are you Arunachala Ramana? Are you God or a *siddha*?" Bhagavan who was living in Virupaksha Cave at the time, replied in verse: "The Supreme Self, the blissful pure consciousness sporting within the heart of all gods and creatures, is Arunachala Ramana"

Ramanachala on the Mount

A quote by Swami:

> Mountain peaks are charming from a distance; when approached, they confront us with terror-striking jungles. So too, the world (*samsāra*) appears charming, when men have not delved into its meaning and value

When i mash this with what Jiddu said while **dissolving** the Order of the Star of the East:

> I maintain that Truth is a pathless land.... Truth cannot be brought down, rather the individual must make the effort to ascend to it. You cannot bring the mountain-top to the valley. If you would attain to the mountain-top you must pass through the valley, climb the steeps, unafraid of the dangerous precipices. You must climb towards the Truth, it cannot be "stepped down" or organized for you,

i was reminded of Ramanachala, who, in one fell swoop, found Himself at the top of the mountain

He didn't ascend; He **transcended**

From His perch, Ramanachala casts His benign glance across the happenings of the world. In some valley, He notices people living by this allusion of the Master:

> A net has been cast into a lake to catch fish. Some fish are so clever that they are never caught in the net. But most of the fish are entangled in the net. Some of them try to free themselves from it. But not all the fish that struggle succeed. A very few do jump out of the net, making a big splash in the water. Then the fishermen shout, "Look! There goes a big one!"
>
> But most of the fish caught in the net cannot escape, nor do they make any effort to get out. On the contrary, they burrow into the mud with the net in their mouths and lie there quietly, thinking, "We need not fear any more; we are quite safe here". But the poor things do not know that the fishermen will drag them out with the net

On yet another crag, He observes a fol"lover" of Steinbeck living by this cool philosophy:

> The hell with it! There ain't no sin and there ain't any virtue. There's just stuff people do. It's all part of the same thing. And some of the things people do is **nice**, and some ain't nice, but that's as far as any man got a right to say

He sees all this with an all-pervading compassionate glance and remains aloof, aloft, immersed in His own joy

Tongue Cleaner

The first thing I do in the morning is brush my teeth and sharpen my tongue~Dorothy Parker

Mid January 2008, **Sai Inspires** had a portion from the mid 1960s:

> The tongue must be sanctified by the repetition of the name. It has also to use sweet expressions which will spread contentment and joy. Be very careful about your speech. Animals have horns, insects have stings, beasts have claws and fangs. But, man's biggest weapon of offence is his tongue. The wounds that his tongue inflicts can scarcely be healed; they fester in the heart for long. They are capable of more damage than even an atom bomb~**Divine Discourse**, July 29, 1964

Later in the day, i was reading about "Captain Courageous" Anil Kumble getting his 600th Test wicket and how it all started: (am proud of him and even more so, as he's a fellow D8C8 in Numbo Jumbo, with a name number adding up to 32)

> **Delighted that Rahul took the catch: Kumble**
>
> In his hour of glory, Anil Kumble forgave even his worst critic who had made a very uncharitable comment about him on his maiden tour of England with the Indian team in

> 1990. Watching a lanky, ungainly 19-year-old Kumble amble across the turf, a renowned former player had quipped, "कहान् कहान् से आजाते हैन् cricket खेल्ने (God knows from where these people turn up to play cricket)"
>
> Kumble, who has never been very athletic, of course, didn't know about this comment then, but came to know much later, decided to close the chapter. "Right through my career there have been a lot of criticism from different quarters, but I have felt that critics are important to egg you on. I hold nothing against anyone", Kumble, who claimed his 600th Test wicket on Thursday, said without naming anyone

The ultimate in not finding fault must be Ramanachala: (**The Power of the Presence**, **Part Two**, page 65)

> Whenever we heard that someone had died, we would make a point of going to sit before Sri Bhagavan because we were all keen to hear Sri Bhagavan compliment the departed person. Even when he talked about people who were, to the rest of us, inveterate scoundrels, he would always find something good to say about them
>
> There was a rich man called Kandaswami who lived in town. Although he occasionally used to come to the ashram for Sri Bhagavan's darshan, the local people detested him because of his bad behavior. During his last days, which he spent in the *manḍapam* opposite the ashram, he suffered from both poverty and disease. While he was lying in this *manḍapam*, he sent word through a

messenger that he would like some gruel prepared in the Malayalam way. Immediately Sri Bhagavan arranged for this gruel to be prepared and sent to him. On the following day Kandaswami's condition became serious, so serious in fact that we were speaking among ourselves, wondering which of his good qualities Sri Bhagavan would speak about when he passed away. A day later, Kandaswami died

We immediately went and informed Sri Bhagavan and sat before him, thinking that even Sri Bhagavan would not be able to think of anything good to say about this man. What a disappointment!

Sri Bhagavan told us, 'No one could keep his body and clothes as clean as Kandaswami. He used neither oil nor soap. He would come at 8 a.m. in the morning and start washing his dhoti. Then he would hang it up to dry. By the time he had completed his bath it would be twelve noon. His hair and beard were always extremely clean'

We hung our heads in shame. Who could equal Sri Bhagavan in seeing only the good qualities in all people?

http://www.go2peru.com/wallpaper.htm

Arunachala's Antipode

From a blog post at the start of 2008 February:

> Bhagavan Ramana Maharshi always insisted that the Holy Hill Arunachala was the spiritual axis of the world, even in a physical sense, similar to the geographical North Pole, with a South Pole axis. So strongly did he maintain the view that another holy hill existed on the opposite side of the globe to Arunachala—which was itself remarkable since he normally did not take very rigid positions except on matters concerning the Self and the Heart— that he once made a devotee pull out a world atlas and look for a similar mountain opposite to Arunachala
>
> The Latitude/Longitude Coordinates of Arunachala are: 12n13, 79e04
>
> There are several striking parallels between the Machu Picchu site and the Shakti culture. The Incas worshiped Machu Picchu as the manifestation of the Divine Mother Goddess of the Universe. They referred to Her as "Pachamama", a name that bears a striking similarity to the name "Pachaiamman" used for Parvathi in South Indian shrines [in the early 1900s, the Maharshi spent many months at the Pachaiamman Temple at the foot of the Hill, outside the town of Tiruvannamalai]. The architecture of the temple city was astrologically and

astronomically determined. Various points of the city serve as a kind of giant sextant or observatory from where specific constellations and celestial objects can be plotted and observed. A closer look at the topology of the city reveals a striking resemblance to the Sri Chakra, the Meru architectural topology that characterizes Indian Shakti shrines

On the psychic plane, multiple individuals with siddhic/occult capacities have separately asserted on visiting Machu Picchu that the city is a place where the feminine aspect of the Universe is especially palpable

Lastly, the Latitude/longitude coordinates of Machu Picchu are: 13s07, 72w34

While the geographical coordinates are not exactly opposite of those of Arunachala, it would be unreasonable to expect it would be exact since the earth is not a precise sphere

There's Plenty of Room in the Itsy Bitsy

*Title inspired by Feynman's talk, **There's Plenty of Room at the Bottom**, given 29.DEC.1959, on the possibilities of NanoTech*

The **Mitchell Beazley Family Encyclopedia of Nature** describes the manner in which DNA works in a very nice way: (page 96)

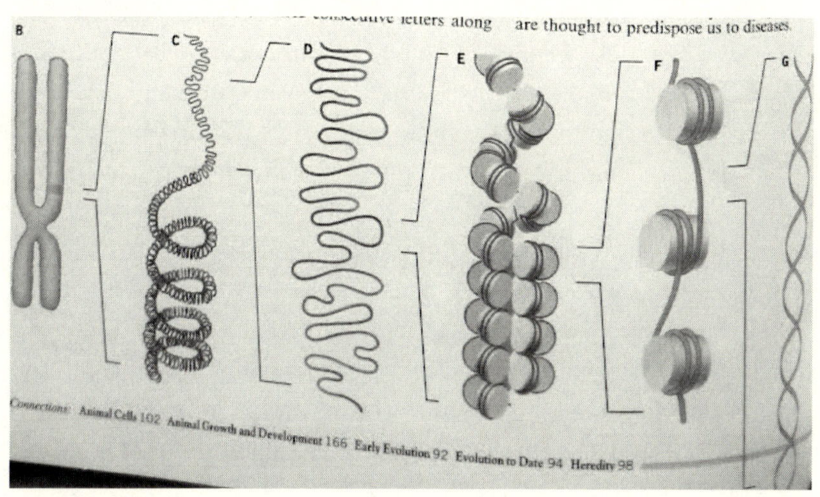

The sidebar above this image goes:

> Viewed under the light microscope, a chromosome of a dividing cell has a simple cross-like shape [**B**] that belies the complex but elegant way in which it "packages" DNA. Magnifying a small section [**C**] reveals a tightly coiled strand of chromatin—DNA closely associated with protein. Further enlarging a segment of chromatin [**D**] shows it to be a tight coil of nucleosomes—bead-like subunits composed of a protein core wrapped by the DNA molecule [**E**]. The protein core is positively charged, allowing it to bind to the negatively charged DNA molecule [**F**] with its double helix structure [**G**]. It is essential to the organization of the cell that the DNA is condensed. If it was not, the DNA double helix would occupy thousands of times more space. By keeping DNA in compact bundles the cell is much better able to manage it, uncoiling certain lengths as the genes contained in them are required

Nature has a way of doing things in the most efficient way. In this case, a sort of zip on demand

Since Incarnations are a reflection of the Formless behind Mother Nature, one would expect them to show similar traits and one is not disappointed. *Sadguru* like Ramanachala and the Master did things **just so** and abhorred waste

There's a sweet anecdote concerning Ramanachala regarding His meticulous way of doing things: (**The Power of the Presence**, **Part Two**, Viswanatha Swami, pp. 237~238)

> Bhagavan was opposed to any sort of waste or extravagance. 'How do you light the fire in your charcoal stove?' he asked me one day
>
> I told him that I used a bit of old rag rolled up and dipped into kerosene. Smilingly, he scolded me for wasting kerosene when the fire could easily be lit with some of the dry twigs and leaves lying around, or with bits of waste paper
>
> On another occasion he saw some small bits of paper, about one inch by six, lying on the floor of Nayana's room and asked him if they were of any use to him. Nayana replied that they were waste pieces. He had been cutting some sheets of paper to a uniform size. These strips were the leftover scraps
>
> Bhagavan said, 'I can stitch these pieces together and make a little notebook the size of a thumb and use it for writing something in'
>
> Nayana beamed with pleasure at this economy, but I, to save Bhagavan the trouble, offered to do it myself
>
> Perceiving my motive, Bhagavan remarked, 'All right, but you are to show me the stitched notebook and the use you make of it'

When I undertook to do so, Bhagavan dropped the matter since he had confidence in my sincerity. As soon as Bhagavan had left I made a tiny notebook out of the bits of paper and wrote down in it the 108 verses of the *Indra Sahasra Nāma Stōtra* and its seven concluding verses that were composed by Ganapati Muni in 1929. This work contains a thousand names of Indra culled from the Rig Veda. Nayana composed this litany of names, adding no other words. 'Indra' refers here, of course, to the Supreme Being, not to the Indra of the Puranas who rises to a godly state by merit and again falls from it

Bhagavan had appreciated the deep, spiritual significance of these names when they had been read out to him during the composition of the work. The next morning, when I showed Bhagavan the tiny notebook with the *Indra Sahasra Nāma* written in it in small script, he scrutinized, as was his way, not only the contents but the stitching and the general appearance as well

He then exclaimed with pleasure, 'You have kept your promise and made the best use of the bits of paper'

The Self in the Pinhole

Read a very unusual thing in a blog post at the end of April 2008:

> **The role of the Heart-centre in Self-realisation**
>
> ...
>
> Saradamma described a small hole in the heart or Heart-centre that the mind had to withdraw into for realisation to take place, saying that when this happened realisation resulted. In the book I summarised what she was telling me about this diagram in the following words:
>
> "As she was explaining this diagram to me Saradamma said that when the mind is just outside the opening one can feel a strong sucking force pulling it towards the hole. She says that the mind is afraid of this force, and that when it feels it, it usually moves away from the hole and tries to escape to the brain. The mind has good reason to be afraid: when it goes through the hole, the Self completely destroys it and Self-realisation results"

The spirit that spoke through Edgar Cayce, my first guru, in a trance was of the view that the soul is allocated to the body at the time of delivery (and **not** at the time of conception) and that it was the Spirit that sustained the fetus from conception to delivery

The above description by Saradamma seems to be bearing this out:

- The Spirit is already in the Heart center (the Cave of the Heart, as Ramanachala put it), and
- After delivery, the mind is occupying the rest of the body and getting the jitters about entering the Heart center, because it's gonna cave in there ;-)

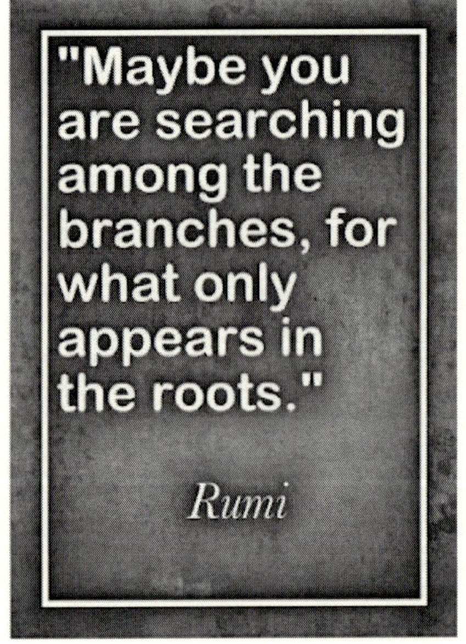

Why Expert Systems Must Fail

I want to know what a man is that he can understand a number, and a number that it could be understood by a man
~Marvin Minsky

At the end of May 2008, on a walk around our gated community, i saw with great clarity why expert systems must fail. The reason is very simple: they do not take Consciousness into account, i.e., they are not **rooted** in Consciousness

The incident that provoked the clarity was this:

On my blog post titled **Born on the Fourth of August** about "Brother Obama", Sammy *sān* had commented:

> **Numbo Jumbo** - What a beautiful phrase! Did you coin it?

Being chastened enough by Ramanachala on who does the thinking / working: (from the end of a mysterious post titled **Half a lifetime ago** by David Godman)

> The feeling 'I work' is the hindrance. Ask yourself 'Who works?' Remember who you are. Then the work will not bind you; it will go on automatically. Make no effort either to work or to renounce; your effort is the bondage. What is destined to happen will happen. If you are destined not to

> work, work cannot be had even if you hunt for it; if you are destined to work, you will not be able to avoid it; you will be forced to engage yourself in it. So, leave it to the higher power; you cannot renounce or retain as you choose. (Maharshi's Gospel, page 5),

i have come to the conclusion that one's mind is nothing more than a **parasite** on Consciousness. So i was reluctant to take credit for that and responded:

> Thank you, Sammy *sān.* **Numbo Jumbo** was one of those phrases which came from the Abyss and presented itself to me. So i don't know whether one can say that one had coined it

To use a holographic example, the abyss of the ocean is the Formless while the waves on it are the form-filled / material aspects of Life. The Formless gives rise to the form; the One becomes the many. Expert systems are designed and developed on equations and interactions **between** the individual waves, while ignoring the most important component of it all, the deep end of the ocean altogether

God is not a toy for your security or a concept for your convenience. God is love. God is the substratum of this universe, the basis of this existence. God is the space in which all things happen
~Sri Sri Ravi Shankar, the Guru of Joy

🄯 Copyleft

Livelihood vs Philosophy

Mid 2008, ran into a Q&A with Suzanne White, the High Priestess of **The New Astrology**, where she made a point of great foresight:

> For years, I have been trying to convince author friends not to sell their electronic rights. I have made many book contracts in my life in many countries and languages. I have never allowed any publisher to own my electronic rights. In the old days, ('70s and '80s before the Net) they were called "audio-visual rights". I always had the feeling they might one day be valuable. So I routinely kept them

So when i saw **The New Astrology** in Google Books, i pinged her, to which she responded:

> Thank you Sastré. I once informed Google they should not use my content online. The Authors Guild here in the States has a lawsuit with them on the subject of copyright. Authors Guild claims the copyright belongs to the author. The publisher usually ignores that and gives Google the right to use the books and to print text from the books
>
> But in my case, the publisher doesn't own the electronic rights. I do

My own response to copyright is quite laid back. Though other bloggers have copyrighted their stuff, i don't feel the need to do so. I think Ramanachala's admonition as to **who** does the work weighs heavily on me. So i replied accordingly:

> For what it's worth, i have a liberal attitude to copyrights. You might call me a copyleft-ist!
>
> I will attribute all the stuff of others properly, but i am lax about my own stuff being used by others. In our philosophy of Advaita, the question is indeed who does things. Ultimately, we believe it is the Great Infinite Spirit that does things; it's just that we get the feeling that we have done it
>
> Though one is not yet 100% there, one would like to keep moving on that path. Hopefully, one can advance from one-sigma (~70%) to two-sigma (~95%) and three-sigma (~99.5%)
>
> Guess it's not surprising that i share my b'day with Tim Berners-Lee, the chap who created the www. If he had copyrighted that, folks say there would have been many mini-webs, but not the wonderful one that we see now

Suzanne White had a very clear-cut response to that, which i couldn't help but appreciate:

> If I were Asian and had studied so much as a smidgen of philosophy, I might be more like you
> ...
> Copyright ensures we get paid for what we do. No matter how spiritual we are, we must eat and feed our families. We don't have any other way to make a living
>
> So bye bye Great Spiritual Being and hello Authors Guild

So i pointed her to David Pogue's:

> **The e-Book Test: Do Electronic Versions Deter Piracy?**

to which she e-mailed:

> Thanks Sastré... David Pogue's forthcoming results are already suspected by my little self because I sell my books as e-books and have been doing so for 4 years. I know about giving away books as opposed to selling them
>
> He and a bunch of other authors (Paul Coelho, for example) are trying this giveaway approach. It is far from stupid to imagine that your hard copy book sales will increase if you give away e-books. I even like the idea and (if I didn't have my own successful bookstore on my web site) I might do it too

> The rub is (and I cannot stress this point enough) that publishers never report what they sell. Perhaps they do tell more or less the truth when they are dealing with a very popular, rich author who (in case he or she doubted the sales reports) might change publishers or audit or even sue them
>
> But for backlisted best-selling authors such as myself who are not rich and have been on their books for over 20 years, publishers somehow manage to sell a suspiciously similar quantity of books every six months and send me a similar check each time

Can't imagine that even popular authors like Suzanne have this challenge

Dad wrote a book on thermodynamics based on his university class notes and all the Macmillan guys ever paid him was a pittance: ₹1,000!

Who Sees?

Found this news item quite intriguing at the end of June 2008:

> **CCTV cameras 'taught to listen'**
>
> CCTV cameras which use artificial intelligence software are being developed to "hear" sounds like windows smashing, researchers have revealed
> ...
> The existing software is sophisticated enough to identify minor visual cues such as whether a car aerial is up or more complex activity such as violent behaviour, researchers said
> ...
> "So, if in a car park someone smashes a window, the camera would turn to look at them and the camera operator would be alerted"

In the late 1980s, read that while humans see an image as a number of sub-images (cues), cameras can only see them as **one full raster** image

It's nice to see the tech catching up. But, of course, it's got a way to go

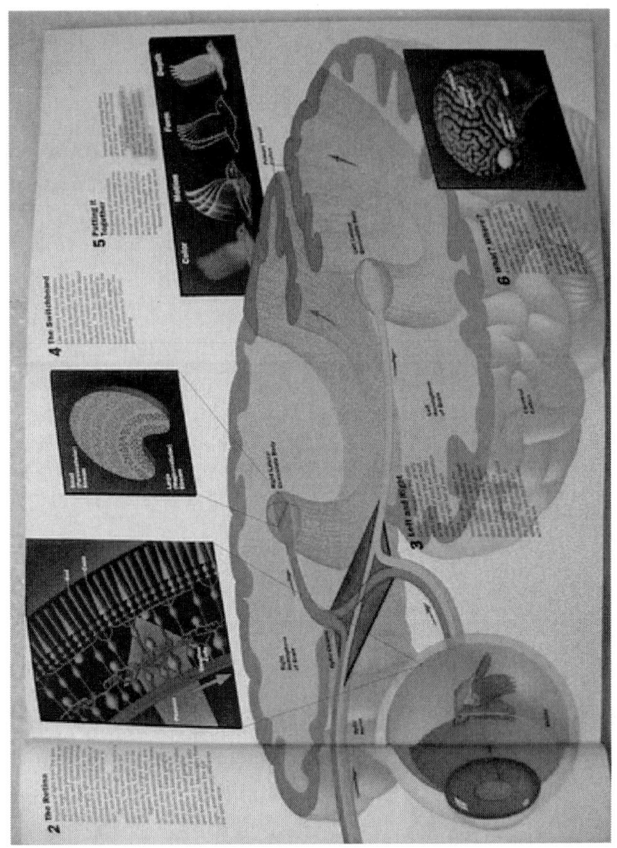

© National Geographic

How are the sub-images/cues that people see converted into a complete image?

That was the subject in an article on the eye in National Geographic Magazine of November 1992, which had a very detailed illustration on how the eye worked [opposite]

To me, the most interesting part was the text at its top right: [highlighted in pink]

> If the brain takes the bird apart, why do we see it whole? For vision scientists that remains a most tantalizing puzzle

Surprisingly i found the answer to this question not in a scientific publication, but in **The Power of the Presence, Part Two**. It is **Consciousness** that puts it all back together. Kunju Swami narrates: (page 28)

> During one of his visits Sri Bhagavan handed him [Narayana Swami] a sheet of paper on which he had just then completed copying **Arunachala Ashtakam**. On that particular day some math heads who knew a lot of Vedanta had also come along with a few other devotees. Narayana Swami read the verses out loud at a slow steady pace so that he could follow their meaning and others could hear him. When he came to the film simile in verse six, he asked Sri Bhagavan for clarification as this analogy was not to be found in the ancient Vedantic works. After hearing Sri Bhagavan's explanation, he understood the import of the verse and also realised the true state of

Bhagavan. The verse, which explains how the mind creates the world, goes as follows:

> You alone exist, O Heart, the radiance of awareness! In You a mysterious power dwells, a power which without You is nothing. From it [this power of manifestation] there proceeds, along with a perceiver, a series of subtle shadowy thoughts that, lit by the reflected light of the mind amid the whirl of *prārabdha*, appear within us as a shadowy spectacle of the world and appear without as the world perceived by the five senses as a film is projected through a lens. Whether perceived or unperceived, these [thoughts] are nothing apart from You, O Hill of Grace

So it's Consciousness that's making us see, but we get the impression that **we** are

The Eternal Student

Read a delicious bit of etymology in the ToI mid-November 2008:

> **Listen Deeply To The Gurbani For Bliss**
>
> ...
>
> The word Sikh in Punjabi is from the verb 'sikhnaa', which means 'to learn'. In a sense, each one of us is a learner throughout our lives

This is one of the great things about the Master. He was an eternal student. The state He kept Himself in, as a child of the Old Mother, was key to that

The other thing was His feeling that the Self was essentially unknowable [Ramanachala had a similar view and discouraged discussions about It]; It can only be experienced to some degree

When Swami Purushottamananda opened the **Gospel** for the very first time, this is what he read: (Chapter **3. Visit to Vidyasagar**)

> "Men often think they have understood Brahman fully. Once an ant went to a hill of sugar. One grain filled its stomach. Taking another grain in its mouth it started homeward. On its way it thought, 'Next time I shall carry home the whole hill.' That is the way shallow minds think. They don't know that Brahman is beyond one's words and thoughts. However great a man may be, how much can he

know of Brahman? Sukadeva and sages like him may have been big ants; but even they could carry at the utmost eight or ten grains of sugar!"

4WRV+FR Ponnampet, Karnataka

Author with Swami Purushottamananda at **Sri Ramakrishna Sharadashrama**, Ponnampet (May 1995)

A few days before, read a very unusual XP: (**Regina's Blog ~ Joy Cures All!**)

> After morning meditation in a cave in the mountain, the chamber in which Ramana lived for several years, I was feeling particularly happy and light spirited. At the end of the walk down the mountain, passing monkeys and pilgrims along the way, I stopped at the ashram for a cool walk through its stony chambers - it was hot outside
>
> As I passed the portrait of Ramana he suddenly became three dimensional, as though he was lifting off the canvas, and smiled at me. I stopped, blinked my eyes a few times and looked again. Again, he lifted off the canvas, smiled and winked. A smile to match his spread across my face as I thought "he's having some fun with me!" Joy filled my heart

When i shared this with a few of my friends, PSM wrote back: (he's a devotee of Paramahansa Yogananda)

> I had a similar experience recently...Portrait becoming 3D
> ...
> Immediately after I finished the evening meditation on the last day, I opened my eyes and my gaze was fixed on Guruji (PY) for some time. I saw the face becoming 3D, i.e., coming out of the photo and giving me a loving smile (I find it very difficult to describe...not exactly fondness or kindness or compassion...the words that came to my mind immediately were – "**I appreciate, I love**")

Felt proud to have a friend with an experience like that!

Such experiences keep one going on this path

The test of a true vision is this: It leaves a lasting spiritual impression on the mind that generates awareness and bliss
~Swami Vijnanananda, direct disciple of the Master

Trip to Tiruchuli

This is a trip that i did with Balan on Saturday 12th November 2005. Early Feb 2009, ran into a kumkum *packet that we got at the beautiful Madura Meenakshi temple, which triggered off wonderful memories of this trip*

Balan was interested in visiting Tiruchuli, the birthplace of Ramanachala. I was keen on visiting a temple in Virudhunagar. So we decided to use Madurai as the base and visit the two places, which are on a sort of isosceles triangle from the temple town

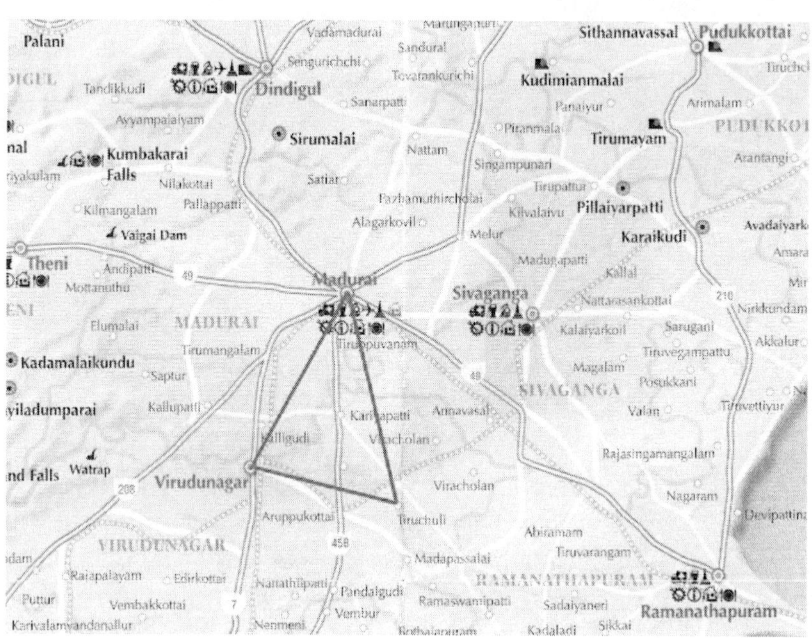

We took a bus from Hosur Road the night of Friday 11th November. Tamil Nadu is connected heavily by good roads, but the ride did get a bit bumpy in the night. We were seated right behind the driver, which added to the tension. Balan told some stories that only accentuated it!

Thankfully, we reached Madurai in one piece and had a nice *chai* to start the day. We then checked into **Royal Court India**, a pretty nifty place. We had a king's breakfast (they had the American plan) and set out for Virudhunagar

The plan was to cover Virudhunagar and Tiruchuli in the morning, come back for lunch, rest for a while, see Mother Meenakshi in the evening, and catch the train back

Organized a cab for the day. Soon we passed by Tirupparamkunram, with the temple to Lord Murugan on a massive hillock

After we landed up at Virudhunagar, it wasn't clear which one had the powerful deity, but we visited a couple of nice temples. Then we set foot in a third one (dedicated to Lord Murugan) and it simply blew me away. Temples in Tamil Nadu are very clean and this one was right at the top

After seeing the main deity (couldn't see His eyes clearly, an important thing for me when visiting a temple), we went around the deities on its periphery. There was a beautiful Nataraja on the left of the entrance, with the *navagraha* right in front of it

There was a Ganesha as well and after we rounded the same, we saw temples to Lord Ayyappa with the 18 steps in miniature, to Goddess Saraswathi, and one to Lord Hanuman, in betel leaves

Then we were in front of the Shiva~Parvathi deities. The Parvathi idol was very imposing and matriarchal. As if not to be outdone, the Shivling was more than three feet tall. I was in a state seeing them both. Then the priest came out and knocked me out. He was at least 6' tall and an *ājānubāhu*, with ultra-long arms. He was like Hanuman, with a thin beard. Seeing a guy like this in the middle of nowhere, my mind was transfixed and i started shedding tears of joy. The priest looked at me quizzically, but i was beyond caring

There was an elephant on the way out, if i recall right

In this warm mood, we set out to Tiruchuli. The temple was sadly quite dilapidated and the house, where Ramanachala was born, was just outside it

From **Bhagawan Ramana Maharshi - Early Years**:

> The 30th of December, 1879 was an auspicious day for the Hindus, the *Ardra-darsanam* day. On this day every year the image of the Dancing Siva, Nataraja, is taken out of the temples in procession in order to celebrate the divine grace of the Lord that made Him appear before such saints as Gautama, Patanjali, Vyaghrapada, and Manikkavachakar. In the year 1879 too, on the Ardra day, the Nataraja Image of the temple at Tiruchuli was taken out with all the attendant ceremonies, and just as it was about to re-enter, Venkataraman was born

We visited the birth-place and gave them a nice donation. Shridi Sai Baba says: (**Shri Sai Satcharita**, Chapter 35)

> Wealth should be the means to work out *dharma*. If it is used for personal enjoyment, it is wasted. Unless you have given it before, you do not get it now. So the best way to receive is to give. The giving of Dakshina advances *vairāgya* [non-attachment] and thereby *bhakti* [devotion] and *jnāna* [knowledge]. Give one and receive tenfold

Then, the priest kindly opened the temple for us. The Old Mother there was lovely. Both of us noticed a cockroach crawling on the deity. The Old Mother, She's crazy about them!

We rested and visited the Madura Meenakshi temple in the evening; very nice it was

After i got back, over a period of time, i found some connections to Virudhunagar:

- The *til* [sesame] oil used in our puja room comes from there; *til* from a place close to the *dil* [heart] :-)
- In the list of STD codes, Virudhunagar comes right before Visakhapatnam

Whenever i think of the trip, the memory of that humongous priest, who looked like Hanuman, makes me cry

Truth is stranger than fiction because Truth doesn't have to stick to possibilities

The Abyss is a Bliss

We need to find God, and he cannot be found in noise and restlessness. God is the friend of silence. See how nature—trees, flowers, grass—grows in silence; see the stars, the moon and the sun, how they move in silence.... We need silence to be able to touch souls~Mother Teresa

In the early 1990s, saw this movie along with my uncle (who has his Ketu in the 12th house; supposed to be an indicator of being in the last life). Both of us enjoyed it immensely

Now i understand the real reason for that joy; the Abyss is the source of all things and beings

https://www.rottentomatoes.com/m/abyss

How long can one enjoy moving around in the surface waters? After a while, it creates a sort of ennui. The real source of joy is deep down

As the Master told Bankim Chandra in the **Gospel**: (Chapter **34. Bankim Chandra**)

> "Let me tell you something. What will you gain by floating on the surface? Dive a little under the water. The gems lie deep under the water; so what is the good of throwing your arms and legs about on the surface? A real gem is heavy. It doesn't float; it sinks to the bottom. To get the real gem you must dive deep"

Ramanachala says much the same thing in **Ramana Maharshi's 100 frequently asked question answers**:

> **64. Question: Am I the froth?**
> Bhagavan: Cease that identification with the unreal and know your real identity. Then you will be firm and no doubts can arise. Because you think that way there is worry. It is a wrong imagination. Accept your true identity with the Real. Be the water and not the froth. That is done by diving in
>
> ...
>
> **68. Question: You often say that there is the real meaning of "I" in the Heart. What does it mean?**
> Bhagavan: Yes, when you go deeper within, you lose yourself as it were in the abysmal depths; then the Reality, which is the Self that was behind you all the while, takes hold of you. It is an incessant flash (or current) of I-consciousness, you can be aware of it, feel it, hear it, sense it, so to say; this is what I call the throb (or current) of the "I"-"I"

Swami alludes: (**Divine Discourse**, May 24, 2002)

> There is plenty of grace that God can give you. But it is at a depth! Some effort is required to obtain it. If you need to fetch water from a well, you need to tie a rope to the bucket, lower it into the well, and draw the water out. The rope to use is that of devotion. This rope must be tied to the vessel of your heart and lowered into the well of God's grace. What you receive, when the water is drawn out, is pure bliss. Live in love with everybody. Once you earn this love, everything else will be added unto you

Of late, i find that i have become indifferent to most things. One stays alone most of the day (with folks away at school), but one is not lonely. Thoughts of the Abyss dominate on the joyous days. One has the feeling of:

> **Just Being, Not Becoming**

Diving deep has another interesting spin-off:

> Conflict reduction

As someone said:

> **You can't argue with Silence**!

In July 2008, we did an interesting painting experiment. As music played, we “danced” with a pencil on a sheet of paper. After a while, we noticed the patterns created by the pencil markings and painted out the stuff. This is what i got

One of my neighbors made an observation that i liked very much:

> There's so much of the paper that hasn't been painted!

Thought it was a very good summary of my state of mind

Realization is a "pinch" away

At the start of April 2009, had a bit of a scary dream: was tailing another guy in a car for some reason and caught up with him after a while. When i accosted him on a bridge, he jumped out of the car, snarled at me like a wildcat, and faded off. Then another guy [in the dream] said that i had bought it as the guy was a dangerous one to mess around with. It was a big relief to wake up

Later, i was thinking: "How come we never think of pinching ourselves when we are in a mess of a dream"? The answer is simple enough: **We don't know that we're in a dream**. Somehow that info [pinching ourselves] hasn't/can't percolate into our dream state; the **rationality** [intellect] bit is switched off in dreams, says Sri Sri Ravi Shankar

We might experience the same thing when we die: “Oh, man, what a relief”!

We might still have to traverse some tunnel in the after-life as the equation might still hold:

Dream : Life = Life : After-life,

but that's OK, all that old life was just a dream :-)

Andy Dufresne, “who crawled through a river of shit and came out clean on the other side”; that’s how i remember **The Shawshank Redemption**

Reflecting your Beloved

While going for the nightly table tennis early April 2009, my kid Marty was mentioning that it was still a Full Moon. I told him that you could see a portion of Swami's face in it. Right after that, a lizard chirped loud and long. We normally regard that as Nature agreeing with our statement. So i was wondering what that meant

If the Universe is a hologram, the Mind~Body~Atma is a fascinating example of this holographic behavior. At the higher level, the MBA maps on to the Moon, Mother Earth, and the Sun. Like so:

Mind : Body : Atma = Moon : Earth : Sun

If the mind in all its glory (i.e., Full Moon) reflects your Beloved, whoever That might be, i guess the objective of life has been achieved

From **The Power of Arunachala**:

> In the second line of the first verse of Sri Arunachala Ashtakam Sri Bhagavan tells us that from his very earliest childhood, when he knew no other thing, Arunachala was shining his mind as the 'most great'

Interestingly, Swami says that the monthly *Shivarātri* (the night before the New Moon) is a very good time to meditate. The reason, of course, is that there's no moon, and hence no mind, and one can easily experience the bliss of the Abyss

As a kid, i used to wonder why the Telugu people held that the Full Moon was the most auspicious time, while the Tamilians gave that status to the new moon; quite like the English and the French bickering!

Now, it's clearer. The Full Moon is the peak of *vidya māya*, while the New Moon is the very depth of "no mind"

The Master refers to Totapuri, His Vedantic guru, in the **Gospel**: (Chapter **22. Advice to an Actor**)

> Nangta used to say that the mind merges in the *buddhi* [intellect], and the *buddhi* in *Bodha*, Consciousness

Is the Universe a Dream of God?

There was a Greek philosopher who used to say that Life was but a dream. One day, he got kicked around badly and some of his tormentors asked him whether he still considered life as a dream. He said: "Yes, but a very painful one"

After reading the experiences of Lakshmana Swamy and that of the Cosmic Consciousness of Swami Vivekananda, am convinced that the Universe is a majestic and mysterious dream of God, differing from ours in very significant ways:

- It's phenomenally long; about 13.7 billion years old
- It's extremely detailed

Ramanachala puts it back on the "seer":

> It is the mind that is vast, not the world. The knower is ever greater than the known, and the seer is greater than the seen. That which is known is contained within the knower, and that which is seen is in the seer; the vast expanse of the sky is in the mind, not outside, because the mind is everywhere and there is no outside to it

That's why we can make some head or tail out of the Universe; it's nothing more than the projection of the Self that powers **our** mind as well

In fact, He says that it's the mysterious power of Consciousness that renders all the objects that one sees in the phenomenal Universe: (**The Power of the Presence, Part Two**: Section on Kunju Swami, page 28)

> In You a mysterious power dwells, a power which without You is nothing. From it [this power of manifestation] there proceeds, along with a perceiver, a series of subtle shadowy thoughts that, lit by the reflected light of the mind amid the whirl of *prārabdha*, appear within us as a shadowy spectacle of the world and appear without as the world perceived by the five senses as a film is projected through a lens. Whether perceived or unperceived, these [thoughts] are nothing apart from You, O Hill of Grace

So the illusion of distance/vastness/separateness is **only** in one's mind

Like people, i feel it's a feature of the Formless that It does not like to be seen in Its naked state for too long :-)

The Master says that one can't keep one's voice on the *ni* (the seventh note) for too long; one has to come back from There. He also says in the **Gospel**: (Chapter **44. The Master on Himself and His Experiences**)

"Further, He revealed to me a huge reservoir of water covered with green scum. The wind moved a little of the scum and immediately the water became visible; but in the twinkling of an eye, scum from all sides came dancing in and again covered the water. He revealed to me that the water was like Satchidananda, and the scum like *māyā*. On account of *māyā*, Satchidananda is not seen. Though now and then one may get a glimpse of It, again *māyā* covers It"

https://plus.google.com/+SwamiVimokshanandaPuri/posts/ihjQvpP3Fby

Premium
Revolutionary Road
twilight
TAKING CHANCE
DEFIANCE
STREET KINGS
YES MAN
SNIPER 3
Premium
Hindi
War
Western

Ramanachala to Surmount

Early August 2009, had converted to a year-long subscription at the DVD shop within our gated community and had been enjoying a spate of wonderful movies, including the Premium ones, which we get to keep for two days instead of the usual one, at no extra cost

Over two days, we knocked back Clint Eastwood's **Changeling** (many twists and turns) and, one afternoon, got **Frost/Nixon**, which i watched for about half an hour over lunch

When we restarted it after dinner, folks started watching from the start and i was wondering what to do. The maid was off from work the next day and the dishes in the sink had to be addressed. With *Shreyas* over *Preyas* [the good before the pleasant] clearly in the mind, i got up to wash them

You can imagine my state; Friday evening, folks watching a neat movie, and me getting my hands dirty! Not an easy one to be in, especially of one's own accord

Then i remembered Ramanachala, who cut vegetables after enlightenment, and it was OK. Soon i was humming:

> *Ramana Sadguru, Ramana Sadguru*
> *Ramana Sadguru, Rāyané*

You can't be sad with a Sadguru ;-)

And, also, this is the great thing about having many Sadguru. You can pick and choose events from Their lives and make yours better

Master Ekkirala Bharadwaj makes a nice comment about that in **Sai Baba The Master**: (page 6, bottom)

> मधुलुब्धो यथा भृंगः पुष्पात्पुष्पान्तरं व्रजेत् ।
> ज्ञानलुब्धस्तथाशिष्यः गुरोर्गुर्वन्तरं व्रजेत् ॥
>
> Just as the bee which is fond of honey moves from flower to flower, the disciple who is fond of wisdom goes from Master to Master~Sree Gurugita

By the time folks got to the point till where i saw, most of the dishes were done and stacked back as well

Frank Langella was absolutely exquisite as the unctuous Nixon and, no wonder, the movie had such a high rating

After it got over, i finished the few remaining dishes; like minds, there are recalcitrant dishes as well. Soak them well and the dirt comes off easily

The Monkey King and I

Late 2009, ran into a few instances of Ramanachala and His simian friends. The first one was this shot:

https://reikiandtheslyman.blogspot.com/2009/01/ramana-maharshi-surrender.html

The next one was in a blog post:

> **Sage Of Arunachala**
>
> ...
>
> Once a group of monkeys were mourning the death of one of their group when Maharishi was on his usual walk. He went and sat with them and explained to them that death is only for the body and not the soul and that they should not weep. The monkeys kept looking at him while he was talking and then walked away
>
> ...
>
> It seems there were a lot of monkeys in Tiruvannamalai and news spread that scientists from some foreign land were planning to come and capture a few of them for their research work. News reached Maharshi and that day when he saw one of the monkeys he sat and talked with him and told him that people were coming to catch them all and if he is intelligent he should escape from here with his group right away. It is indeed amazing that when the scientists did arrive and search around for monkeys they could not get even a single monkey all around Tiruvannamalai in spite of searching all day

There was one in the chapter of the (lovely) experiences of Rangan with Bhagavan: (**The Power of the Presence**, **Part One**, pp. 22~23)

> Crows, dogs, monkeys, squirrels, sheep and many other animals came to see Bhagavan. Many of them instinctively recognized his benevolence and greatness, had his darshan and went away. It is the human being alone who uses his intelligence and thereby fails to recognize Bhagavan's greatness. When we look at Bhagavan through the distorting prism of our minds, we think that Bhagavan is some ordinary, insignificant person
>
> Monkeys frequently visited Skandashram to play in the trees and to visit Bhagavan. Once, when I had come from Madras for darshan, a whole tribe came to visit. One of the monkeys approached Bhagavan, sat in his lap and embraced him. The monkey looked like he was giggling. He also seemed to be saying something to Bhagavan
>
> Bhagavan remarked, 'The monkey is telling me that today he has been accepted as the king of the monkeys. Look at the monkeys sitting on the wall. That one is the queen, the first lady of the kingdom. Over there is the second, junior queen'
>
> Then, pointing out some of the others, he continued, 'The chief of his army is sitting there. All the others are his soldiers'

There were nearly a hundred monkeys assembled there. In their joy and excitement they climbed the trees, broke many of the branches, jumped around and made a lot of noise

Bhagavan stroked the monkey king's head and said, 'The lame boy has become a king today. He has come to give me the good news'

Since some of the devotees did not know the story of Nondi, 'the lame boy', Bhagavan told us again for their benefit

'This monkey was a boy when I was in Virupaksha Cave. One day the other monkeys bit him, inflicted many wounds on him, and departed, leaving him behind. The poor boy came to me with all his wounds, so I looked after him till he recovered. Even then I knew that one day he would become the king. It has happened today. Usually monkeys do not accept a monkey that has been looked after by a human being, but this one was accepted back into the tribe after it had recovered'

Suri Nagamma writes in **Face to Face with Sri Ramana Maharshi**: (Section 39)

A few days later, I wrote four verses under the title '*Prārthana*' and placed them before Bhagavan. Seeing them he began to laugh to himself. Noticing this, Bhagavan's another attendant Rajagopala Iyer asked what had been written. With a smile he said, "These four verses are written as a prayer. The second verse is amusing. It seems, after I left the hill and settled down here, I have no monkeys to serve me. So, 'why not accept my mind which is a monkey for service? This monkey is after material things. Tie it down or chastise it; but see that it does service to you.' Adi Sankara in Sivananda Lahari has written a *slōka* approximating to the idea, wherein he says: 'O, Lord Sankara! You are a *bhikshu*. Why not tie down my mind, known as monkey, to your stick and go about begging? You will then get alms in abundance'"

FACE TO FACE WITH
SRI RAMANA MAHARSHI

(Enchanting and Uplifting Reminiscences of 160 persons)

Sri Ramana Kendram, Hyderabad

Shaving the Man in the Mirror

They say that when you buy a book, you should also be able to buy the time required to read it :-)

Many books languish on the shelves before one gets around to reading them. I distinctly remember the time required to complete **The Razor's Edge**; finally i got around to reading it late at night in a hotel room at Tirupati. What a lovely feeling it was when i got around to finishing it

The same happened with **Face to Face with Sri Ramana Maharshi**

This is an exquisite book. How long can one on the Self remain on the shelf?

G Lakshmi Narasimham writes : (Section 106)

The essence of what Bhagavan said in my talks with him was:

"You say that on final analysis all that I see or think or do is one; but that really comprises two notions: the all that is seen; and the 'I' that does the seeing, thinking, and doing, and says 'I'. Which of these two is the more real, true, and important? Obviously the seer, since the 'seen' is dependent on it. So, turn your attention to the seer who is the source of your 'I' and realize it. This is the real task. Up till now you have been studying the object, not the subject. Now find out for what reality this 'I' stands. Find the entity which is the source of the expression 'I'. That is the Self, the Self of all selves"

This direct, simple teaching was like a tonic to me. It swept away the unrest and confusion that till then had haunted my mind

The experiences of Prof. GV Subbaramayya include a very neat explanation (and pun!) on creation: (Section 41)

> Dr. Syed, Professor of Philosophy, Allahabad University, asked Bhagavan, "What is the purpose of creation?" Usually Bhagavan gave replies in Tamil, Telugu, or Malayalam. This time He spoke directly in English, and asked, "Can the eye see itself?" Dr. Syed replied, "Of course not. It can see everything else, but not itself". To Bhagavan's question that "if it wants to see itself", he said, "It can see itself only in a mirror". Bhagavan then commented, "That is it. **Creation is the mirror for the 'I' to see itself**"

So the Universe, majestic and mysterious, is an **appearance** in this I, the Self

On the futility of learning (too many) things in this world, R Narayana Iyer has a very illustrative experience: (Section 100, **boldfacing** in original)

> Once a few very learned Sanskrit scholars were seated in the hall discussing portions of the Upanishads and other scriptural texts with Bhagavan. I felt in my heart, how great these people are and how fortunate they are to be so learned and to have such deep understanding and ability to discuss with our Bhagavan. I felt miserable. After the pandits had taken leave, Bhagavan turned to me and said, "What?" looking into my eyes and studying my thoughts, "This is only the husk! All this book learning and capacity to repeat the scriptures by memory is absolutely of no use. Not by reading do you get the Truth. **Be Quiet**, that is Truth. **Be Still**, that is God"
>
> Then very graciously he turned to me again, and there was an immediate change in his tone and attitude. He asked, "Do you shave yourself?" Bewildered by this sudden change, I answered trembling that I did. "Ah", he said, "For shaving you use a mirror, don't you? You look into the mirror and then shave your face; you don't shave the image in the mirror. Similarly, all the scriptures are meant only to show you the way of Realization. They are meant for practice and attainment. Mere book learning and discussions are comparable to a man shaving the image in the mirror". From that day onwards my long-standing sense of inferiority vanished once for all

For folks who use *nāma-smarana* as a way to the Self, the experience of Kavyakanta Ganapati Muni is very educative: (Section 91)

> Ganapati Muni, a great Siva bhakta, chose Tiruvannamalai, the holy seat of Siva, for his *tapas* in 1903 and briefly met Sri Ramana on the hill. In 1907, when he came again to Tiruvannamalai he found that nothing tangible had emerged from his severe tapas. Disappointed, he climbed up the hill and fell flat on his face holding Sri Ramana's feet with both hands. With a voice trembling with emotion he cried, "All that has to be read I have read. I have performed *japa* to my heart's content. Yet I have not up to this time understood what *tapas* is. Pray, enlighten me about the nature of *tapas*"
>
> After listening to the Muni, Sri Ramana silently gazed at him as he sat in anxious expectation. Then he said in Tamil, "If a *mantra* is repeated and attention directed to the source from where the *mantra*-sound is produced, the mind will be absorbed in that. That is *tapas*". This short instruction filled Muni's heart with joy. He stayed on the hill for some hours and composed five stanzas in praise of the Swami in which he shortened his original name Venkataraman to 'Ramana', which has stuck to the Swami ever since

Ramana Sadguru, Ramana Sadguru
Ramana Sadguru Rāyané

Arunachala in Google Earth

Eons of Arunachala

You don't have to be the biggest or the best, if you're the first
*~Seen in **The Sunday Gentleman** by Irving Wallace*

If Ramanachala was attached to anything, it was to just the Hill

In **Face to Face with Sri Ramana Maharshi**, we find Ramanachala saying: (Annexure 1)

> "Someone from abroad wants a stone from the holy part of the hill. He does not know that the whole hill is holy. The hill is Lord Siva Himself. As we identify ourselves with the body, so Siva has chosen to identify Himself with the hill"

Read a snippet as well that might give some factual basis to the mythological story of Arunachala appearing as a column of fire: (Annexure 1)

> The word 'Annamalai' in Tamil means 'an inaccessible mountain'. 'Annal' is a special name for Lord Siva, who appeared in this place in the form of a column of fire, neither the top nor root of which could be approached, hence inaccessible. The mountain thus came to be known as Annal Malai (*malai* in Tamil means mountain). Slowly the word got corrupted to Annamalai. Paul Brunton, in his **A Message from Arunachala**, writes that his geologist friend from America held the view that Arunachala was thrown up by the earth under the stress of some violent volcanic eruptions in the dim ages before even the coal-bearing strata were formed

That was a very long time ago!

The Carboniferous [https://g.co/kgs/vk1XTT], during which coal was produced, is a geologic period...that spans 60 million years from the end of the Devonian Period 358.9 million years ago (Mya), to the beginning of the Permian Period, 298.9 Mya

Follow the Teaching

I will follow the advice of my guru,
even though he might smoke hemp
~Sri Ramakrishna

After the brouhaha over Swami Nithyananda, have been getting a number of messages poking fun at him. It's easy to kick a person when he's down

Am reminded of that observation by Jesus:

> “Let he who is without sin cast the first stone”

and its corollary:

Why worry about what Swami Nithyananda has done? Let us concentrate on ironing out one's own challenges

As Ramanachala observed:

> The greatest gift you can give the world is your own realization of the Self!

Incidentally, it was in a Nithyananda newsletter that i read:

> See understand: Desire and gratitude can never coexist. When you feel one desire after another, it means that you are not living with gratitude. When you live with gratitude, you can never have any desires. When you live with gratitude, whatever is given to you will simply fulfill whatever you need at that moment, that's all. Even before you ask, you will be given, so there will be no question of asking!

This was very nicely summarized by Dr. Thimappa Hegde in his wonderful Valedictory address for my kid's class at Greenwood High at the end of January 2010:

> "You can never be grateful and miserable at the same time, can you?"

Much To-Do about Nothing

People are forever telling me, "Please do this if you are not doing anything", but they don't understand that doing nothing is exactly what i want to be doing
~From an old Reader's Digest

One of the things about hanging around home from 2006 has resulted in my inability to understand folks who are forever seeking something to do, something to finish. They are on a perpetual adrenaline rush and seek completeness in some work done. If you removed the work component out of them, it's as if they'd just collapse, as Maugham writes in **The Razor's Edge**:

> Marionettes that the showman had thrown into the discard

The ocean-wave metaphor for the Self seems to be much more in the background. The wave seeks to split away from the ocean, but it can only do so, to an extent. Then why struggle so much?

The state we call realization
is simply being oneself,
not knowing anything
or becoming anything

Simpler to follow the injunction of Ramanachala:

Be still and know that you are God

To do is to be~Socrates
To be is to do~Sartre
Doo bee doo bee doo~Sinatra
Scooby dooby doo~Hanna-Barbera

Girivalam with Gopa ~ 2010

Triggered off the idea of this trip with Gopa, my childhood pal, in September 2009. It took some time to happen but, live in the Now and things will take care of themselves

Day 1: Wednesday 24th November 2010

Our first stop on the way was at the **Om Shakthi MahaGanapati temple**

I had two miraculous experiences in the vicinity of the Ganesha here [https://flic.kr/p/4CBbK] and make it a point to take *darshan* while traveling in the direction of Hosur, south of Bengaluru

VM93+WG Bengaluru, Karnataka

Later, we saw this 4+1 with the insignia of Lord Venkateswara right alongside

41 is a very mysterious number in Numbo Jumbo and Lord V keeps drawing that number to Him

Incidentally, **Tiruvannamalai** also adds up to 41 in Numbo Jumbo

Around this time, i was telling Gopa about how the **Gospel** and **The Power of Arunachala** use the same metaphor (cow tied down by a rope) in different ways:

Gospel: (Chapter **47. The Master's Training of His Disciples**)

> DOCTOR: "I do not say that the will is absolutely free. Suppose a cow is tied with a rope. She is free within the length of that rope, but when she feels the pull of the rope-",

while in **The Power of Arunachala**, we read:

> The spiritual benefits of *pradakshina* have been described by Sri Sadhu Om in one of his Tamil poems, *Sri Arunachala Pradakshina Manbu.* In verses six and seven he says, 'A cow grazing round and round its peg, does not know that the length of its rope is thereby decreasing. Similarly, when you go round and round Arunachala, how can your mind know that it is thereby subsiding? When the cow goes round more and more, at one point it will be bound tightly to its peg. Similarly when the mind lovingly goes more and more round Annamalai [Arunachala], which is Self, it will finally stand still in Self-abidance, having lost all its movements [*vritti*]'

Soon, we had the first sight of Arunachala:

63F5+FF Tiruvannamalai, Tamil Nadu

Gopa with Sukha Brahma

After a while, we went to the **Akaash Sesha Bhavan** and had some tea outside. A wandering mendicant came over. He spoke in Telugu and told us that his name was Sukha Brahma. He was selling flowers/fruit in Koramangala, Bengaluru when he chucked it all up and became a wandering *sannyāsi*

I wondered whether i could ever do something like that and go on that Ma Narmada Parikrama!

Then we got back to the SRM Old Age Home and had this sight:

62FW+CP Tiruvannamalai, Tamil Nadu

Arunachala from SRM Old Age Home

Balan mentioned that *aksharamanamālai* [The Marital Garland of Letters] would be sung on Wednesdays at 5:50 PM

We walked to Sri Ramanasramam and got a bit delayed, reaching there only around 6 PM

Deepam on Arunachala was a sight

63F4+FM Tiruvannamalai, Tamil Nadu

Deepam on Arunachala from **Sri Ramanasramam**

Gopa found the Tamil [of *aksharamanamālai*] very soothing

I had the same feeling when i heard it first. I joined in on the refrain: ... *Arunachala*

After that, there was some more chanting in the main hall. Thought there was a possibility of seeing David Godman, Michael James, or Richard Arunachala. I went behind one Westerner and muttered, "Richard", but that didn't make an impression on him. Later, one of my pals mentioned that Michael James was away in London, but he did see David Godman that evening, who might have been the guy i tailed in vain

Told Gopa about the unusual experience of Lakshmana Swamy with the Ganesha in the temple dedicated to Ramanachala's Mother in **Sri Ramanasramam**

Details are in the earlier *girivalam* with Balan in 2007

63F4+FM Tiruvannamalai, Tamil Nadu

Then we saw the other places (not too many) in the ashram

Unusually, met a friend from Infosys while in front of the MahaNirvana room

63F4+FM Tiruvannamalai, Tamil Nadu

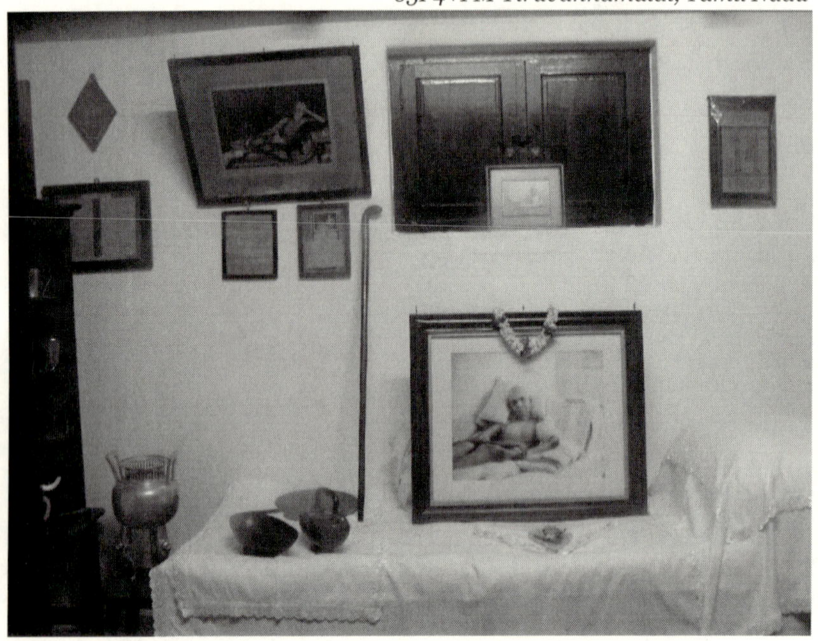

MahaNirvana room at **Sri Ramanasramam**

The center-piece photo is by none other than Henri Cartier-Bresson, that exponent of the Decisive Moment!

We walked across to **Akaash Sesha Bhavan**; they were now open but serving only snacks for dinner

We were ravenous and did full justice to the options available

At the counter, there was this Ganesha on a tree!

63F5+FF Tiruvannamalai, Tamil Nadu

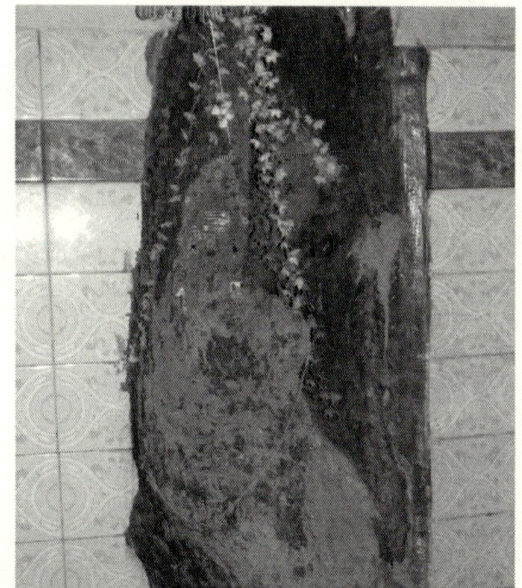

We made our way back to SRM Old Age Home in the dark and chatted with Balan for a while

The issue of *samskāra* (impressions) came up with a simple example: a guest in your house has chucked **his** towel onto **your** bed. What do you do?

That word **mine** is a loaded one, in more ways than one!

Day 2: Thursday 25th November 2010

Even though we slept in a bit late, i was up by 05:35 and held up Gopa with my morning routine (facing the south face of Arunachala), during which he read a book in the doorway from the light of the lamp in the loo!

While freshening up, played the *Arunachala aksharamanamālai*. Whether you understand them or not, the lyrics tend to get under your skin. Gopa was mentioning that the same had been running over and over in his head since he heard them the earlier evening. I have had the same effect for the past few weeks

When we got out, there was this sight of swirling stuff:

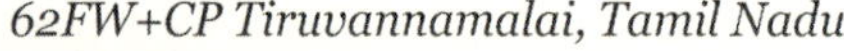
62FW+CP Tiruvannamalai, Tamil Nadu

SRM Old Age Home

and an idol of Ramanachala facing His beloved mountain

We dropped in on Balan and he gave me a couple of oranges, which i promptly put away and asked for more like, well, Oliver Twist. One of the challenges of the morning was to ensure that you finish the ab-loo-tions for the day, with so much travel coming up down the pike: the *girivalam* and the drive back to Bengaluru

Gopa & self headed out to Akaash Sesha Bhavan and dug in to some *pūri* and *pongal*

Soon we were ready to go around Arunachala

We bade goodbye to Balan, on his cycle!

We were walking on the right (to face the oncoming traffic, better to get hit from the front than from behind) single-file

You might have read about how the four-minute mile was cracked: John Landy set the pace for Roger Bannister [wearing jersey #41], who took over at the end. We sort of followed the same idea. Gopa was more keen on walking, while i like to photograph. So he'd maintain his speed (he once finished 10 km in 80 min!) and, once i took my photos, i'd **run** to catch up with him. That ensured that we finished the 14-km *girivalam* walk in 2½ hours

Some notes on *girivalam*: (from **The Power of Arunachala**)

- In one verse often pointed out by Sri Bhagavan, Jnanasambandhar described this hill as being *jnāna-tiral*, a dense mass of *jnāna*
- 'Bhagavan, who scarcely ever gave advice to devotees unless asked, wholeheartedly encouraged their going round the hill as conducive to progress in *sādhana*', writes Lucia Osborne
- Sri Bhagavan told him, 'For everybody it is good to make a circuit of the hill. It does not even matter whether one has faith in this *pradakshina* or not; just as fire will burn all who touch it whether they believe in it or not, so the hill will do good to all those who go round it'
- Sri Bhagavan said to Kunju Swami, 'This hill is the storehouse of all spiritual power. Going round It benefits you in all ways'
- 'Bhagavan used to say that if one went round the hill once or twice, the hill itself would draw one to go round it again. I have found it true. Now this is happening to Dr. Syed', writes Devaraja Mudaliar in **Day by Day with Bhagavan** (19th December, 1945)

You run into this **Shri Valampuri Vinayagar** temple when the *girivalam* path peels off from the highway and the tiled *girivalam* path starts

62HR+CH3, Tiruvannamalai, Tamil Nadu

Be patient like the Nandi, says Isha Sadhguru

The tiled path made the walk pretty easy, though it didn't run throughout; they are still working on it

I enjoyed running into this sadhu who reminded me of this later:

The Power & Significance of Mount Arunachala

Millions of Siddha masters live at Mount Arunachala in their Light Body form. When you walk around Mount Arunachala, you can commune with these ascended masters and receive their grace and blessings. Occasionally, you may have the good fortune to encounter such masters who appear to you in a physical form disguised as beggars or wandering monks seeking alms or food

This is the reason that Ramanachala would ask folks to walk on the **outer** periphery (left of the path) of Arunachala, the **inner** periphery (right of the path) being reserved for these masters

62QJ+7MH, Athiyandal, Tamil Nadu

Soon we were in front of this wonderful **Thiru Ner Annamalai Temple**

Heard that it is bang opposite the big temple on the other side of the mountain – the *girivalam* path is not exactly circular

Gopa was quite intrigued by the tools that were on display along the way (this had the most)

after which we saw the rugged North Face of Arunachala

Contrast this with the south face, which reminds me of peace and Mt. 11:28:

> *Come to me, all you who are weary and burdened, and I will give you rest*

We were back in the town now and walking was that much more difficult but, to compensate, there were some funky sights, including a kid pissing nonchalantly right in the middle of the street!

We went straight through at the one temple that i saw dedicated to Lord Venkateswara and landed near the **Arulmigu Arunachaleswarar Temple**, which has a lot of detail

63J9+M3 Tiruvannamalai, Tamil Nadu

The lion was the marker for peeling off from the highway, back to SRM Old Age Home

We hung around with Balan for a while and started back for Bengaluru around noon

అరుణాచలా మజాకా? (Arunachala Magica?)

Sometime back, saw some radical stuff:

> **Deepak Chopra says there there is no way to prove existence of an outside world**
>
> Any neurologist will assure you that the brain offers no proof that the outside world really exists and many hints that it doesn't...
>
> The cortex doesn't inform us about this never-ending data processing, which is all that is happening inside gray matter. Instead, the cortex tells us about the world—it allows us to perceive sights, sounds, tastes, smells, and textures—the whole array of creation. The brain has pulled an enormous trick on us, a remarkable sleight of hand, because there is no direct connection between the body's raw data and our subjective sense of an outside world

This dovetailed very neatly with that orthogonal **Superparadigm** article by Peter Russell, which **convinced** me of the Formless:

> **All that I see, hear, taste, touch, smell and feel has been created from the data received by my sensory organs.** All I ever know of the world around are the mental images constructed from that data. However real

and external they may seem, they are all phenomena within my mind

What happens when some of the sensory organs go kaput? There's a very interesting experience on that:

Expansion and Dr. Jill Taylor's Talk

Are Brains Wired for Enlightenment?

A stroke shut down half of a brain scientist's brain. Cornered in the other half, she plunged into a samadhi-like state of love, bliss and insight

---

Albert Einstein observed that the most **incomprehensible** thing about the Universe was that it was comprehensible. But, if it's all happening **within**, there's really no big deal about understanding it

This was why Ramanachala said:

"It's not the Universe that's vast but the human mind"

Sri Nisargadatta Maharaj took it one step further with His searing observation in **I Am That**:

"I am not a part of the world; the world is a part of me"

So how does one see things? Ramanachala says: (**The Power of the Presence, Part Two**: Section on Kunju Swami, page 28)

> You alone exist, O Heart, the radiance of awareness! In You a mysterious power dwells, a power which without You is nothing. From it [this power of manifestation] there proceeds, along with a perceiver, a series of subtle shadowy thoughts that, lit by the reflected light of the mind amid the whirl of *prārabdha*, appear within us as a shadowy spectacle of the world and appear without as the world perceived by the five senses as a film is projected through a lens. Whether perceived or unperceived, these [thoughts] are nothing apart from You, O Hill of Grace

If you feel all this is a load of baloney, here's a simple test. The next time you fall into deep sleep and wake up fully refreshed, try to ascertain **where** you were during that period. You can't, because your mind was **totally subsumed** into your (spiritual) Heart. No mind [*manōnāsha*] for a while; only the I and Its accompanying Bliss

In fact, reading the above by Ramanachala makes me realize why Arunachala is regarded as the *sahasrāra chakra*

In his work **The Magical Revival**, Kenneth Grant writes of Arunachala as one of the global *chakra*:

> "The supreme seat of energy - the Sahasrāra Chakra - is not located within the physical body at all, but above the cranial suture, where, figuratively speaking, the Lotus of Infinite Light blooms and bathes with its perfume the

subtle anatomy of man. The Sahasrāra is the seat of the Atman, the True Self in Man which is known as the Brahman in the Cosmos. It is the Abode of Siva and is represented on earth by the Sacred Hill of Arunachala in South India. This is the cult-centre of the most profoundly spiritual Path now open to humanity, i.e., the *advaita-mārg* or Path of Non-duality"

https://arunachalagrace.blogspot.com/2011/10/kenneth-grant-on-arunachala.html

Paramahansa Yogananda meets Ramanachala

After Edgar Cayce, my first spiritual guru, i was drawn to Paramahansa Yogananda (PY). I had even subscribed to Kriya Yoga by post, though i never got around to actually doing it

So it was quite nice to know that PY met Ramanachala in 1935 on his travels through Bharat

Here are a couple of interactions from **Talks with Sri Ramana Maharshi** that PY and his secretary have with Ramanachala (indicated as **M.** in the talks):

Friday 29th November, 1935

Talk 106

Swami Yogananda with four others arrived at 8.45 a.m. He looks big, but gentle and well-groomed. He has dark flowing hair, hanging over his shoulders. The group had lunch in the Asramam

Mr. C. R. Wright, his secretary, asked: How shall I realise God?
M.: God is an unknown entity. Moreover He is external. Whereas, the Self is always with you and it is you. Why do you leave out what is intimate and go in for what is external?

D.: What is this Self again?
M.: The Self is known to everyone but not clearly. You always exist. The Be-ing is the Self. 'I am' is the name of God. Of all the definitions of God, none is indeed so well put as the Biblical statement "I AM THAT I AM" in EXODUS (Chap. 3). There are other statements, such as *Brahmaivaham*, *Aham Brahmasmi* and *Soham*. But none is so direct as the name JEHOVAH = I AM. The Absolute Being is what is - It is the Self. It is God. Knowing the Self, God is known. In fact God is none other than the Self

D.: Why are there good and evil?
M.: They are relative terms. There must be a subject to know the good and evil. That subject is the ego. Trace the source of the ego. It ends in the Self. The source of the ego is God. This definition of God is probably more concrete and better understood by you

D.: So it is. How to get Bliss?
M.: Bliss is not something to be got. On the other hand you are always Bliss. This desire is born of the sense of incompleteness. To whom is this sense of incompleteness? Enquire. In deep sleep you were blissful: Now you are not so. What has interposed between that Bliss and this non-bliss? It is the ego. Seek its source and find you are Bliss. There is nothing new to get. You have, on the other hand, to get rid of your ignorance which makes you think that you are other than Bliss. For whom is this ignorance? It is to the ego. Trace the source of the ego. Then the ego is lost and Bliss remains over. It is eternal. You are That, here and now.... That is the master key for solving all doubts. The doubts arise in the mind. The mind is born of the ego. The ego rises from the Self. Search the source of the ego and the Self is revealed. That alone remains. The universe is only expanded Self. It is not different from the Self

D.: What is the best way of living?
M.: It differs according as one is a *jnāni* or *ajnāni*. A *jnāni* does not find anything different or separate from the Self. All are in the Self. It is wrong to imagine that there is the world, that there is a body in it and that you dwell in the body. If the Truth is known, the universe and what is beyond it will be found to be only in the Self. The outlook differs according to the sight of the person. The sight is from the eye. The eye must be located somewhere. If you are seeing with the gross eyes you find others gross. If with subtle eyes (i.e., the mind) others appear subtle. If the eye becomes the Self, the Self being infinite, the eye is infinite. There is nothing else to see different from the Self

He thanked Maharshi. He was told that the best way of thanking is to remain always as the Self

Talk 107

Later the Yogi asked: How is the spiritual uplift of the people to be effected? What are the instructions to be given them?
M.: They differ according to the temperaments of the individuals and according to the spiritual ripeness of their minds. There cannot be any instruction *en masse*

D.: Why does God permit suffering in the world? Should He not with His omnipotence do away with it at one stroke and ordain the universal realisation of God?
M.: Suffering is the way for Realisation of God

D.: Should He not ordain differently?
M.: It is the way

D.: Are Yoga, religion, etc., antidotes to suffering?
M.: They help you to overcome suffering

D.: Why should there be suffering?
M.: Who suffers? What is suffering?

No answer! Finally the Yogi rose up, prayed for Sri Bhagavan's blessings for his own work and expressed great regret for his hasty return. He looked very sincere and devoted and even emotional

Hovering Dreams and Dreaming of Arunachala

In the early 2010s, had been thinking of the Great Arunachala that much more. When i do the *nāma japa*, i think of this manifestation of Shiva on Earth. Incidentally, Ramanachala's admonition in **Who am I?** is of immense help:

> 14....Without yielding to the doubt "Is it possible, or not?", one should persistently hold on to the meditation on the Self

One morning got a hovering dream. While flying dreams involve flying at heights at speed, the hovering dream is of a more placid variety where one is floating three to four feet in the air

I was in some sort of airport lounge, with a great deal of space. Initially, i was hovering only for a little while, kicking off the walls to lengthen the time spent in the air

Then i developed a trick of running for a while and then hop-skipping into the air. That got me to stay longer airborne without having to hang around close to the walls. All very mysterious *vis-à-vis* the life we are accustomed to, but pretty much OK in dreams; anything goes in dreams!

After some time of this tomfoolery in the air, most of my family members got together along with some foreigners in the same airport lounge. It was now much more packed, but i was still up to these tricks. When someone wondered how it was being done, a Russian lady interjected: "There's nothing to it"!

Dreamt of Arunachala one morning at the end of June 2012

Was traveling with family and other relatives. During a break, i went outside and saw the Great Arunachala. It was much more humongous. The eyes were playing tricks. See with the left, It would appear to the right; see with the right, It would appear to the left, displaced significantly. Can never explain dreams, though we never question that in the dreams themselves; the rationality bit is switched off!

As **William C. Dement** (what a name!) said:

> Dreaming permits each and every one of us to be quietly and safely insane every night of our lives

Anyway, the "snout" of Arunachala, aka Parvati Hill, was that much more pronounced. It was in fact the highest point in my view

Parvati Hill

62FW+CP Tiruvannamalai, Tamil Nadu

Probably, It was saying that i should concentrate on the Old Mother, who's anyway my favorite

© **Zeb Andrews** https://flic.kr/p/8wFty8

Arunachala the Gateway

One night, at the end of May 2012, i couldn't sleep. So, got up and read an **entire** issue of Geo, the French magazine closest to National Geographic Magazine

It had an interesting pic of a naturally-formed hole in the wall in Copper Bay, South Africa [https://goo.gl/maps/jDUYimhKjVq3kTmB8]

I had recently blogged something called the **iHole in the Wall**, so was thinking it was a good photo to add at the bottom of that post. But when i googled for the same, couldn't find anything remotely like it

So i switched to the next best source, Flickr, and got some neat photos tagged “hole in the wall”

To me, the best of the lot was, of course, this masterpiece by Zeb Andrews (opposite, above)

After some time, it struck me that the upper portion of the profile looked so much like Arunachala, the rugged view looking west, the so-called Murugan Face; you don’t mess with the Zohan!

In a sense, it was a vindication of what Michael James writes in **The Power of Arunachala**:

> That is, so long as we identify the body as 'I', it is equally true that this hill is God. Indeed, Sri Bhagavan used to say that because we identify the body as 'I', Lord Siva, the Supreme Reality, out of his immense compassion for us, identifies this hill as 'I', so that we may see him, think of him and thereby receive his grace and guidance. 'Only to reveal your [transcendent] state without speech [i.e., through silence], you stand as a hill shining from earth to sky', sings Sri Bhagavan in the last line of the second verse of **Sri Arunachala Ashtakam**

Through Arunachala, one can experience the Formless

Guru Tvam

In the **Shri Sai Satcharita**, some qualifications are listed for brahma-jnāna (or Self-Realization): (chapters 16~17)

> (9) The necessity of a Guru. The knowledge of the self is so subtle and mystic, that no one could, by his own individual effort, ever hope to attain it. So the help of another person-Teacher, who has himself got self-realization is absolutely necessary. What others cannot give with great labour and pains, can be easily gained with the help of such a Teacher; for he has walked on the path himself and can easily take the disciple, step by step on the ladder of spiritual progress

There's an amusing interaction on the same topic from **Face to Face with Sri Ramana Maharshi**: (Section 79; MA Piggot was the first English lady who visited Ramanachala)

> One day we brought up the question of guruship and asked, "Is it necessary for spiritual attainment to have a guru?" The Maharshi ordered a certain treatise to be read, in which it was stated that as in all physical and intellectual training a teacher is sought, so in matters spiritual the same principle holds good. "And", he added, "it is hard for a man to arrive at the goal without the aid of such a one". I turned to him and said, "But you had no guru"

A rustle of shocked horror ran through the hall. But the Maharshi was not in the least disturbed by my thoughtless remark. On the contrary, he looked at me with a twinkle in his eye. Then he threw back his head and gave a joyous whole-hearted laugh. It endeared me to him as nothing else could. A saint who can turn the laugh against himself is a saint indeed!

https://realization.org/p/ramana/gallery-notes/wp/wp_24.html

Go, Delusion

Found a very interesting response from Richard Dawkins in an interview with Playboy (of all things!), which was trending on **The Browser** some time back:

> PLAYBOY: Assume there is a god and you were given the chance to ask him one question. What would it be?
>
> DAWKINS: I'd ask, "Sir, why did you go to such lengths to hide yourself?"

My respect for Mr. Dawkins went up quite a few notches. He's an atheist in the same league as that other Richard [Feynman]

We see similar ideas in various scriptures:

> Truly Thou art a God who hidest Thyself
> ~Isaiah 45.15
>
> No vision can grasp Him,
> But His grasp is over all vision;
> He is above all comprehension,
> Yet is acquainted with all things
> ~Quran 6.103

I asked the Messenger of God, "Did you see thy Lord?" He said, "He is a Light; how could I see Him?"
~Hadith of Muslim

The eye cannot see it; the mind cannot grasp it.
The deathless Self has neither caste nor race,
Neither eyes nor ears nor hands nor feet.
Sages say this Self is infinite in the great
And in the small, everlasting and changeless,
The source of life
~Mundaka Upanishad 1.1.6

From the **Gospel**: (Chapter **4. Advice to Householders**)

M: "When one sees God does one see Him with these eyes?"

MASTER: "God cannot be seen with these physical eyes. In the course of spiritual discipline one gets a 'love body', endowed with 'love eyes', 'love ears', and so on. One sees God with those 'love eyes'. One hears the voice of God with those 'love ears'. One even gets a sexual organ made of love"

At these words M. burst out laughing. The Master continued, unannoyed, "With this 'love body' the soul communes with God"

M. again became serious

From **Face to Face with Sri Ramana Maharshi**: (Section 41. GV Subbaramayya)

> Dr. Syed, Professor of Philosophy, Allahabad University, asked Bhagavan, "What is the purpose of creation?" Usually Bhagavan gave replies in Tamil, Telugu, or Malayalam. This time He spoke directly in English, and asked, "Can the eye see itself?" Dr. Syed replied, "Of course not. It can see everything else, but not itself". To Bhagavan's question that "if it wants to see itself", he said, "It can see itself only in a mirror". Bhagavan then commented, "That is it. Creation is the mirror for the 'I' to see itself"

The Universe, majestic and mysterious, is thus an appearance in the Self and created in **play**. We mustn't take it too seriously

Ramana *means* ***one who plays***

Was very intrigued by this pic and line by Christo in the **Voices** section of the November 2006 issue of NatGeoMag:

"All our projects are absolutely irrational with no justification to exist. Nobody needs a running fence or surrounded islands. They are created because Jeanne-Claude and I have this unstoppable urge to create. They are made for us first. Not the public"

https://pin.it/13Qv8lX

Heck, the Self must have thought the same when It created this Universe, and probably many others

Reminds me of this stunning discussion from the **Gospel**: (Chapter **22. Advice to an Actor**)

> MASTER: "This world is the *līlā* of God. It is like a game. In this game there are joy and sorrow, virtue and vice, knowledge and ignorance, good and evil. The game cannot continue if sin and suffering are altogether eliminated from the creation"
>
> ...
>
> HARI: "**But this play of God is our death**"
>
> MASTER (smiling): "**Please tell me who you are**. God **alone** has become all this-*māyā*, the universe, living beings, and the twenty-four cosmic principles. 'As the snake I bite, and as the charmer I cure'. It is God Himself who has become both *vidya* and *avidya*. He remains deluded by the *māyā* of *avidya*, ignorance. Again, with the help of the guru, He is cured by the *māyā* of *vidya*, Knowledge"

The Learned and the Realized

There's a line in **Shri Sai Satcharita** that always startles me. GS Khaparde was a noted lawyer, but he **never** opened his mouth before Shirdi Sai Baba, because: (Chapter 27)

> Learning cannot shine before Self-realization

Something similar between Ramanachala and Ganapati Muni in **Face to Face with Sri Ramana Maharshi**: (Section 91)

> Ganapati Muni, a great Siva *bhakta*, chose Tiruvannamalai, the holy seat of Siva, for his *tapas* in 1903 and briefly met Sri Ramana on the hill. In 1907, when he came again to Tiruvannamalai he found that nothing tangible had emerged from his severe *tapas*. Disappointed, he climbed up the hill and fell flat on his face holding Sri Ramana's feet with both hands. With a voice trembling with emotion he cried, "All that has to be read I have read. I have performed *japa* to my heart's content. Yet I have not up to this time understood what *tapas* is. Pray, enlighten me about the nature of *tapas*"
>
> After listening to the Muni, Sri Ramana silently gazed at him as he sat in anxious expectation. Then he said in Tamil, "If a mantra is repeated and attention directed to the source from where the mantra-sound is produced, the mind will be absorbed in that. That is *tapas*". This short

> instruction filled Muni's heart with joy. He stayed on the hill for some hours and composed five stanzas in praise of the Swami in which he shortened his original name Venkataraman to 'Ramana', which has stuck to the Swami ever since

Like the Universe, there's no end to learning, and its associated challenge: pride of all that learning. Ramanachala is quite categorical about the futility of this in ***Nān Yār?***:

> **21. Is it necessary for one who longs for release to inquire into the nature of categories (*tattva*)?**
>
> Just as one who wants to throw away garbage has no need to analyse it and see what it is, so one who wants to know the Self has no need to count the number of categories or inquire into their characteristics; what he has to do is to reject altogether the categories that hide the Self. The world should be considered like a dream

The only Real thing is the Self and, if we are interested in That, we should pursue it with one of its tethers: the **Who am I?** inquiry or, for those interested in other means, ***nāma***

These are the threads by which one can reach the Self. Of course, they might not be long enough for That purpose, but as Ramanachala Himself vouchsafed, if you go down deep enough into the Abyss, the Self will on Its own pull you in into Its Hadal fold. A different type of string theory ;-)

Sri TS Chandran

Brahmachaitanya Maharaj used to say, "We shouldn't need to tell the name of our Guru. People should be able to recognize our Guru from our behavior". Do we realize how big this responsibility is!~KV Belsare

Early April 2013, Sridhar from our avenue was telling me about his uncle, Justice Sri TS Chandran, with whom he stayed for some years early on in life

At the age of 22, Sri TS Chandran had the great privilege of being with Ramanachala the last six years of His life!

His actions mirrored those of Bhagavan: never giving advice unless asked for, doing rather than talking, no work (like giving early-morning coffee to Sridhar and waiting to take the used cup back) being "too low". Once Sridhar got up early and found him meditating. That was his daily routine, from 4~6 AM

Sri TS Chandran (1922~2011)

Very similar to what Prof. NR Krishnamurti Aiyer observed about the daily life of Ramanachala, in **Face to Face with Sri Ramana Maharshi**: (Section 48)

- Personal cleanliness
- Tidiness of dress
- Habitual wearing of *vibhuti* and *kumkum* on the forehead
- Equal sharing of all enjoyment with those around him
- Strict adherence to a time schedule
- Performing useful work however 'low' it may be
- Never leaving a work unfinished
- The pursuit of perfection in every action
- Incessant activity except while sleeping or resting after a spell of hard work
- Never considering oneself superior to others
- Speaking the truth always, or strict silence if the expression of truth would hurt or lower the reputation of others
- Perfect self-help
- Never asking another to do a piece of work which can be done by oneself
- Taking full responsibility for failure, if any, without shifting the blame on others
- Accepting success or failure with equanimity
- Never disturbing the peace of others
- Leaving the leaf-plate clean after eating
- Complete non-interference in the affairs of others
- Never worrying about the future

Nirbhayankara

*This is from the time [2012]
when the Nirbhaya case rocked the country*

There was a message on our AUCoE mailing list first thing in the morning:

> With dismay and shame about being an Indian, cannot help but cringe thinking about the agony, pain, and helpless torture that ... is going through in Delhi right now...

Couldn't quite get what he was referring to. As i later tweeted:

> @timesofindia the one good thing about your full-page ads is that i don't get to see the muck on the front page; i read from the Sports page

Like Earl Warren:

> I always turn to the sports pages first, which records people's accomplishments. The front page has nothing but man's failures

Wonder what one can really do about it. How does one control the actions of others when our own don't seem to be within ours?

Even if one does something about it, how does one prevent a recurrence? As **The Catcher in the Rye** says:

> If you had a million years to do it in, you couldn't rub out even half the "F... you" signs in the world. It's impossible

And while you're at it, someone will sneak up and write one right under your nose! So, this can't be solved looking outward. Which is why Ramanachala said:

> Your own self-realization is the greatest service you can do to the world

What happens when you attain that? You will see the world as a dream, appearing **within** the context of the Self

Later, after the nice Sufi music and lunch at a friend's place, hit the deep end of the ocean. Woke up and felt blissful. Things going awry take longer to irritate :-)

What happens in deep sleep? The little i gets sucked into the Big I. It's not much different from *samādhi*, except that one is unaware of it. One can feel its aftereffects, though. It is for this reason that Ramanachala categorically asks:

> If the everyday world exists by itself, why doesn't it show itself in deep sleep?

It can't, because the world depends on the seer, pun intended, for its existence

Aortic Valve Repair

I was born with a **bicuspid** aortic valve (AV)

What that means is that, instead of three leaves that fully close the AV after the heart pumps blood to the body, there are only two leaves. So there's a bit of leakage and the pumping operation is not 100% efficient, resulting in **aortic stenosis**

We discovered this in 1976 when some doctors visited our Kotak Salesian school in Vizag. I was the only one detained for further examination. That was when we discovered the bicuspid bit

In the early 1980s, when 3D echocardiograms were available, we investigated further at NIMS, Punjagutta in Hyderabad. The doctors said that the critical parameter was the **gradient** and that was the one to be monitored over time

Over the next many years, we took our eye off this ball and it was only around the end of 2012, the supposed end of the world, due to random severe dizzy spells that we realized the gradient had gone into the critical areas

Doc Bijay Kumar Mahala, the consultant at Narayana Hrudayalaya, now Narayana Health, on Hosur Road did an angiogram (CAG) mid-January 2013 and said that it was better to get operated pronto

We delayed that for a while and met Doc Devi Shetty at the start of May 2013

Doc Shetty was in one corner of a very spacious room, with the CD of the angiogram playing on a 32" LCD TV next to him. He was in his surgeon garb and very charming

He had a quick look and said that it was better to get cracking and complete the Aortic Valve Replacement (AVR). That was a similar conclusion we were coming to, considering that it was a sort of a one-way ticket and there was no chance of it getting any better

With the high gradient, the heart was exerting itself so much more to get the requisite pressure beyond the AV. He opened up a 3D model heart to make it simple for us. Due to my young (!) age, the tissue valve couldn't be used for replacement and one had to go for a metallic valve

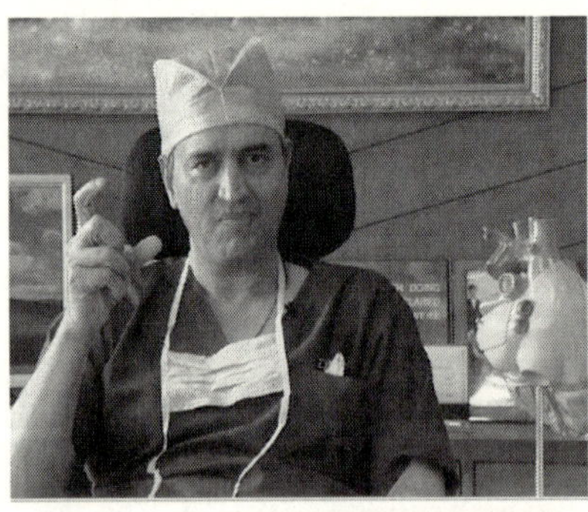

http://healthymagination.com/about/advisory-board/devi-prashad-shetty

In between, he put a very reassuring hand on my forearm

He was just a week away from his 60th birthday and i wished him in advance

Am still kicking myself for not taking a photo with/of him, but this is a very similar image

All that pain of waiting dissolved after that quick meeting. Quite similar to seeing the imperious Emperor [Lord Venkateswara] at Tirumala, whose chants (Om Venkatesaya Namaha) were going on in the background, all through our discussion. He asked us to take it further with Surgeon/Doc PV Rao

We couldn't meet Doc PV Rao that evening, but his secretary, who gave us his business card. Doc PV Rao's on Gmail and, from that, saw his YouTube channel. He seemed to be a follower of Ramanachala!

We could meet the surgeon only in the afternoon the next day, in his 3rd floor cabin

While chatting, looked up and saw a painting of Ramanachala. Haven't seen anything like that before; a Google Search didn't reveal anything similar, it was a "gnarled" version of what you normally see

Surgeon PV Rao said that there was a 1 in 5 chance of just cleaning up the AV and making it as good as old. However, they still had to open up the heart and **then** make that call

The mechanical valve comes with its own set of challenges:

> However, current mechanical heart valves all require lifelong treatment with anticoagulants (blood thinners), e.g. warfarin, which requires monthly blood tests to monitor

Call that warfaring with warfarin

https://www.thehindu.com/society/history-and-culture/ramana-maharishi-many-endearing-dimensions/article31389221.ece

While leaving, saw another large photo of Ramanachala, which was facing the doc. Had a very quick peek, but it looked like this

Thanks to the Ramanachala connection, all my apprehensions **dissolved** on meeting Surgeon PV Rao

Felt that i was in very safe hands

As the day of the AVR approached, it was a good test for my idea that:

Spirituality = Philosophy in Action

Two sources of apprehension:

- Whether the dizzy spell would act up **during** the AVR
- Whether i would remember all my passwords post surgery! Wrote the important ones down for good measure

After the angiogram in January, the insurance company flatly refused to pay for the operation, citing some non-disclosure from my side way back in 2007

Insurance companies are ever ready to take money from you, but it's very tough to get it back

As Brooks tells Andy in **The Shawshank Redemption**:

> Son, six wardens have been through here in my tenure, and I've learned one immutable, universal truth: Not one of them born whose @sshole wouldn't pucker up tighter than a snare drum when you ask them for funds

So had to raise the substantial funds for the AVR operation on my own

But Ramanachala was really looking after me that month: Some money that we deposited with the Income Tax Department way back in Dec 1999 got released **that** month and the **interest** over 14 years was just enough to meet the expenses for the AVR!

Earlier, in February, Michelle sent me this "reading":

> I finally have some quiet time to get a decent email back to you. I have felt/seen your chakras waiting most patiently and this time they're not alone. There's a man I see who says he is your "uncle", but this might be a term used in a symbolic way as the face I saw was Sri Ramana Maharshi
>
> He watches over you and he's smiling. He touched one hand to his forehead, the centre of roughly third eye area. Then he sat down, cross legged. I asked him if there's anything he wants me to tell you. He held out a stick, in both hands he's holding it out about shoulder height. It's shorter than a walking stick, maybe a metre in length and it looks like wood bound on one end with string or cord, pale raw cotton coloured cord. It's for you
>
> He puts words in my head one by one and I typed them that way. He "said":
>
> "Tell him that his days are numbered like the stars, every one is there for a purpose and to glorify the many faces of the Creator. Nothing is by chance, not death or destruction. Your illness is a part of your journey. It will leave you when that journey is done and only then. No medication can alter this path for you. Do not be afraid"
>
> Then he smiled and sat back. I asked about the "journey is done" and got told that this means a life lesson, not necessarily that you'll be ill till you die, but that you'll be ill

until this lesson, this "journey" had been accomplished. He nodded slowly, smiling

Faith is to believe what you do not see;
the reward of this faith is to see what you believe
~Saint Augustine

With so much Grace, went in fearlessly for the AVR on a date where all its parts were Fibonacci numbers:

Tuesday 21st May '13

I checked with the nurse, who was administering the anesthesia, whether there was any danger of the dizzy spell occurring during the AVR. She was dismissive about it, which was very reassuring

Then it was lights-out for a couple of days as i was sustained on the heart-lung machine; got lucky as the AV just had to be **cleaned**

Hustled the good Doc to discharge me by that Saturday (25th May) and he obliged. He even presented me **Upadesa Saram** in Telugu, written by Sri Devisetty (!) Chalapathi Rao

Two devotees of Ramanachala

I limped back to normal over the next couple of months, and could play serious badminton from early August. The baddy folks were zapped, but i was very clear:

It was a miracle of Arunachala

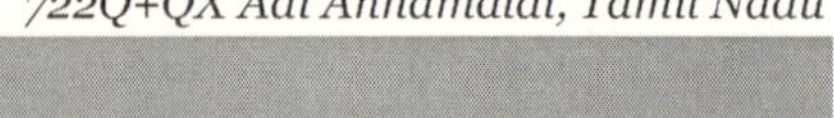
722Q+QX Adi Annamalai, Tamil Nadu

Arunachala from **Adi Annamalai Temple**

Very unusually, if you could see Arunachala from Bengaluru, this is the view you get, as the line of sight passes through Adi Annamalai Temple

The Underlying Reality

Mid May 2013, my pal VSS sent me a Scientific American article:

> **Leonard Susskind: The Bad Boy of Physics**
>
> Physicists seeking to understand the deepest levels of reality now work within a framework largely of Susskind's making. But a funny thing has happened along the way. Susskind now wonders whether physicists can understand reality

In the interview, to the question:

> In the midst of all this remodeling, is there room for such a thing as an objective reality?

he responds:

> ...So I say, let's get rid of the word "reality". Let's have our whole discussion without the word "reality". It gets in the way. It conjures up things that are rarely helpful. The word "reproducible" is a more useful word than "real"

Incidentally, "reproducible" is more or less the same word that Susskind's friend (Feynman, whom he refers to in the last question of the interview) uses when he talks of the miracles at Lourdes

Peter Russell wrote a lovely article, which convinced me of the Formless, on this underlying Reality that we can never get to first base with:

> **Reality and Consciousness: Turning the Superparadigm Inside Out**
>
> The fact that we create our image of reality does not mean, as some people misconstrue, that we are creating the underlying reality. Whatever that reality is, it exists apart from our perception of it. When I see a tree there is something that has given rise to my perception. But I can never directly perceive this something. All I can ever know of it is the image appearing in my mind

We can probably grasp and play around with the **mirror** of Reality that's happening in our heads, but there's no way we can understand what's Really "out there"

Ramanachala would generally discourage all discussion on the underlying Reality, the Self

If the everyday world exists by itself,
why doesn't it show itself in deep sleep?
~Ramanachala

How to Chant *nāma*

There's a nice pointer on how to chant *nāma* in the *pravachan* of Sri Brahmachaitanya Maharaj for May 21, the day i got operated:

> **Exert Yourself to Remember nāma**
>
> There is no *sādhana* so subtle and yet so gross as *nāma*. One who wants to say anything most earnestly, says, "I tell you this from the bottom of my heart (or, literally 'the navel')". So *nāma*, too, should be taken from the bottom of the heart, or the navel, because all desires spring from there. When it is made the seat of *nāma*, it will gradually dislodge desire and totally extinguish it in the end. *nāma* should be practised not superficially, casually, but sincerely and insistently. Let us not worry as to how we shall respond to sensuous pleasures when all desire becomes extinct

The navel (solar plexus, to be exact) is, of course, the location of the *maṇipūra chakra*. In his immensely readable **Travels** (both outer and inner), Crichton writes that this *chakra* is highly developed in Westerners. I tend to think of it as the *chakra* of *rajas* [the innate tendency or quality that drives motion, energy and activity], and the seat of desires. Annihilate desires through *nāma* and see what happens

maṇipūra chakra
https://en.wikipedia.org/wiki/Manipura

Ramanachala gives a slightly-different focus to Kavyakantha Ganapati Muni for chanting *nāma* in **Ramana Periya Puranam**: (pages 51~52)

> Kavyakantha leapt out of the hollow. It was one o'clock in the afternoon, and the sun was beating down hard. The *Kārthikai* festival was on and hundreds of people thronged around the hill. Undeterred, he ran up the hill to Virupaksha cave and found Bhagavan sitting alone outside. Bhagavan directed his glance of grace at Kavyakantha. Like many devotees before him, he was transfixed and could not take his eyes off Bhagavan. Kavyakantha, an erudite scholar, had never prostrated himself before any human being. Suddenly, he found himself flat on the

ground in front of the young ascetic. He held Bhagavan's feet tightly and cried, "I have read all that has to be read. I have fully read Vedanta, I have performed *japa* to my heart's content, yet I have not understood what *tapas* is! Therefore, I have sought refuge at your feet. Pray, enlighten me as to the nature of *tapas*". The word *'tapas*' in Sanskrit literally means 'striving for the realization of truth through penance and austerity'. However, Bhagavan imparted its deeper meaning to Kavyakantha. Helping him rise to his feet, Bhagavan looked into his eyes and after some time slowly replied, "If one watches from where the notion 'I' arises, the mind is absorbed into that. That is *tapas*". And since Kavyakantha had himself revealed that he practiced mantra *japa* - repeating mantras thousands of times every day, the master added, "When repeating a mantra, if one watches the source from which the sound is produced, the mind is absorbed in that. That is *tapas*"

To me, this appears to be the *anāhata chakra*, close to the location of the spiritual heart on the right

anāhata chakra
https://en.wikipedia.org/wiki/Anahata

He who turns inward with untroubled mind to search where the consciousness of 'I' arises, realizes the Self and rests in thee Arunachala, like a river when it joins the ocean
~Arunachala Pancharatnam

On Time

Time is that funny thing that prevents everything from happening at the same time

My interest was piqued by Dennis Overbye writing in the NYTimes, **A Quantum of Solace**, where he refers to a new book, **Time Reborn: From the Crisis in Physics to the Future of the Universe**

So many books, so little...time

The part that made the most sense to me was:

> John Archibald Wheeler, the visionary Princeton physicist who was Bohr's disciple, once pointed out that the future and the past are theory. They exist only in records and the thoughts of the present, a fulcrum, in which all stories end and begin

This is what sages and folks like Eckhart Tolle have been dinning into our heads with books like **The Power of Now**

Consider a place where one has, say, goofed up. Whenever one is there, there's a twinge of regret how one could have avoided that mistake. But there's nothing one can do about it. You're in the same place, but not in the same time. That's why they say corny things like "You can't step in the same river twice"

As we have seen earlier, the world of name and form (space-time) comes with the Formless. It can't exist by itself. They are like two sides of a coin, where the head wags the tail, unbeknownst

But why do we see the world, in the first place?

When the mind separates itself from its source; in the same manner as the sphere becomes an ellipsoid

From **Delta of Delight**:

> 'Lingam' means that in which all things merge and out of which all things emerge. The Absolute, the Ultimate Reality, Brahman or God has no opposites, no polarities, no contradictions, so, it is represented by the most perfect mathematical symbol, the sphere. When the basic desire, *Ekoham Bahusyām*, 'I am One, let me become many', disturbs the perfect balance of the One, the sphere divides itself into two, we get the ellipsoid. The lingam is ellipsoid. The One Brahman has become Siva-Sakthi, the primary polarity principle of the positive and negative

http://www.crystalheartbooks.com/blog/?p=9

When the mind sinks back into the Self, in the Cave of the Heart, the world ceases to exist

Types of Samadhi

Deep Sleep	Mind alive; sunk in oblivion
Kevala	Mind alive; sunk in Light
Sahaja	Mind dead; resolved into the Self; like a bucket with the rope left lying in the water in a well, to be drawn out by the other end of the rope; like a river discharged into the ocean and its identity lost; a river cannot be redirected from the ocean.

First-hand experience of this is common: a siesta. You sleep for just a little while, maybe just ten minutes, but you wake up, all refreshed, to take on the entire evening

That's why Ramanachala said:

> Your own self-realization is the greatest service you can do to the world

Because, when you wake up from the dream called Life, do you worry about all the others who were there in the dream along with you?

Some have said: Yes! They are the Incarnations :-)

Mater, not Pater

Do you look on God as Father or Mother?

My natural tendency is similar to that of the Master, look on God as Mother Kali or Mā Narmada

From the very inspirational reminiscences of Prof. GV Subbaramayya in **Face to Face with Sri Ramana Maharshi**: (Section 41)

> The next day Bhagavan casually narrated the story of Mira Bai's visit to a well-known *swāmi* in Mathura, whose disciples refused her permission for *darshan* on the ground that their guru did not meet women. Mira Bai observed: "I thought that there is only one *purusha* [her Giridhar Gopal] and all the rest of us are women". When these words were communicated by the disciples to the guru, he at once realised that Mira Bai was a *jnāni*, and he came out and saluted her

The catechism of the Catholic Church indicates a similar thing: that all nuns are mystically betrothed to Jesus Christ

It's not at all surprising that the big Dudes of Hinduism have a feminine angle

The most beautiful picture of Lord Venkateswara that i have seen looks like a lady to me

via WhatsApp

Had read about the experience of Swami Brahmananda at Tirumala: (**God Lived With Them**, page 106)

> In Tirupati Maharaj [Swami Brahmananda] saw the Divine Mother in the image of Lord Venkateswara. His body shivered in ecstasy. Later he said to Sharvananda: "I have distinctly seen the form of the Divine Mother. Please inquire about it". After inquiry and close examination of the image and sanctuary, it was found to have been originally a Shakti temple, later converted into a Vishnu temple, probably under the influence of Ramanuja

Am more and more inclined to believe that the Old Man at Tirumala is actually the Old Mother in disguise. She's much closer to my heart, anyway

Arunachala has a similar aspect

From the section on Kavyakanta Ganapati Muni in **Ramana Periya Puranam**: (page 52)

> A little known secret about Arunachala is that the front is the Father aspect while the back is the Mother aspect. All miracles and powers - psychic, spiritual, physical or worldly - stem from the Mother aspect. In the lives of Bhagavan's devotees, miracles and visions took place between *Nirudhilingam* [in the south-west] and *Eshanyalingam* [in the north-east]

62FW+CP Tiruvannamalai, Tamil Nadu

Arunachala from **Sri Ramana Maharshi Old Age Home**

A Slightly Different Preposition

Know thyself, then, to be as a corpuscle, as a facet, as a characteristic, as a love, in the body of God
~Edgar Cayce Reading 2533-7

One of my favorite reads as a kid in the late 1970s was **I am Joe's Body**, featured in Reader's Digest, and then later on available as a Berkeley edition for just ₹29. It had some very intriguing stuff on cells:

> Surprisingly, the DNA in the rod cells of Joe's eyes contains all the information needed to produce a complete baby! The DNA in an ear cell could theoretically construct a foot. We don't do these nonsensical things because in each of us large portions of the DNA template are blocked out. My DNA makes rod cells, nothing else

I think it's the same with people. Some are destined for greatness while others have to function as the back "orifice"

I like to imagine the solar system as a humongous body of the Self of which we are all parts. One of my pals, the man behind SwanandAshrama in Bengaluru, once had a vision on those lines

With two of our WIMWI batchmates, Raghuram Rajan and Nachiket Mor, hitting the big league at RBI and the Gates Foundation in the mid-2010s, i like to visualize them as the eyes of the Old Man, bright, scintillating, and in the limelight

Even though i was known as NVS at WIMWI, thankfully i have little of that. I was cured of it when my junior and D10 dorm-mate, KV Srinivas, who was sort of in the same league as Raghuram Rajan, got injured in the head by the rugged knee of one of our classmates while playing football, became a vegetable, and later died :-(

We are all facets in the body of the Self. If we are content wherever we are (placed), it's the road to peace and, who knows, perhaps self-realization!

David Godman concludes his remarkable tale of coincidences in **Half a lifetime ago** with:

> The feeling 'I work' is the hindrance. Ask yourself 'Who works?' Remember who you are. Then the work will not bind you; it will go on automatically. Make no effort either to work or to renounce; your effort is the bondage. What is destined to happen will happen. If you are destined not to work, work cannot be had even if you hunt for it; if you are destined to work, you will not be able to avoid it; you will be forced to engage yourself in it. So, leave it to the higher power; you cannot renounce or retain as you choose (Maharshi's Gospel, page 5)

So, work is done **through** you, not **by** you. A minor change in preposition, but a world of difference in the end result

IMHO, if you open yourself up as a channel, much more good will flow through you

Linda Goodman wrote in detail on this aspect, wrt to money, in **Star Signs**, but you can extend that principle to many other things

Ajāta

First tie the knot of non-dual knowledge in the corner of your cloth; then do as you please
~Sri Ramakrishna

Of late i am getting more and more drawn to *ajāta*:

> There is no creation, no destruction, no bondage, no longing to be freed from bondage, no striving to be free [from bondage], nor anyone who has attained [freedom from bondage]. Know that this is the ultimate truth
> ...
> Though Guru Ramana, who appeared as God incarnate, expounded numerous doctrines, as befitted the different states and beliefs of the various devotees who sought refuge at his feet, you should know that what we have heard him affirm to intimate devotees in private, as an act of grace, as his own true experience, is only the doctrine of *ajāta* [non-creation] (Guru Vachaka Kovai, verse 100)

Detachment

Of all the spiritual ideas, this has had the maximum effect in weakening my hold on the world. And live with more detachment, in a *sāttvic* manner (this is, of course, my personal choice)

If the world is arising in our Consciousness only because of the mind being separated from the Self residing in the Cave of the Heart (more in this in **On Time** earlier), then it makes sense not to get too attached to it and live with, hopefully, a *gossamer* touch. After all, it's just a figment of my (and of everyone else's) imagination

And it becomes more possible to follow that great observation by Swami Vivekananda:

> One should be able to attach and detach at a moment's notice

The Amway guy got more than he bargained for when he called up my Infosys friend PVBala:

> AmGuy: Hi, would you like to make more money?
> PVBala: No

Living Life without Angles

As a kid, it was in **The Sunday Gentleman** that i first came across the idea of an angle for a story. Figure out the writer's angle and you know where the story is heading. But i haven't been able to live Life that way

Paramahansa Yogananda says that the Self is "Center Everywhere, Circumference Nowhere". With such a picture, there are **no** angles
Find this more in sync with my behavior; say it as it is and get on with Life. That might not work well in everyday life, but the

Master reassuring a devotee in the **Gospel** is a great inspiration: (Chapter **28. At the Star Theatre-I**)

> "You are generous and artless. One cannot realize God without sincerity and simplicity. God is far, far away from the crooked heart"

Would rather live closer to God, the underlying Reality, rather than the world

> *Sell your cleverness and buy bewilderment~Rumi*

But don't be a **bore** while doing so! Enjoy Life, as the Master says in **How to Live with God**: (page 443)

> Once, explaining his wide-ranging interests, the Master said: "I don't like to be monotonous. I would like to make a bouquet with **five** kinds of flowers. I would like to play a flute with **seven** holes in it. I would like to taste various kinds of food. I don't want to be a dry monk"

Sri Arun Lele once sent me a very interesting quote that, seeing us in action, people should be able to guess our Guru :-)

Going Home

And when the time comes for us to "go home", it will be easier to follow what Khushwant Singh wrote so elegantly in his **10 rules for living**; i like to think of them as **The Ten-ets**:

> Above all, when the time comes to go, one should go like a man without any regret or grievance against anyone. Iqbal said it beautifully in a couplet in Persian: "You ask me about the signs of a man of faith? When death comes to him, he has a smile on his lips"

Everyone is so afraid of death, but the real Sufi just laughs: nothing tyrannizes his heart. What strikes the oyster shell does not damage the pearl
~Rumi

Gunayana

Or, Rama sattva

After fifteen years as a stay-at-home Dad, one thing i notice is the lessening of *rajas* in everyday life. Content prevails over form. There's no need to dress up for work or for anyone. No one to kowtow to. There's no traffic & road rage to contend with

Though it's not as much as i would like it to be, there's more of *sattva* in one's life, esp. if i have a good siesta in the afternoon. The mind gets cleared of all the gunk and the evening is pure pleasure. Reactions are muted, one is more being (rather than becoming), going with the flow of the Self

Ramanachala says that *sattva* is a precondition for experiencing bliss. Unless the waves are stilled in the mind, how can the sun be reflected in all its pristine glory?

We read, in ***Nān Yār?***:

> **12. Are there no other means for making the mind quiescent?**
>
> ...
>
> Of all the restrictive rules, that relating to the taking of *sāttvic* food in moderate quantities is the best; by observing this rule, the *sāttvic* quality of mind will increase, and that will be helpful to Self-inquiry

And, thanks to my general tendency to prefer *shreyas* over *preyas* [the good over the pleasant], i steer clear of *tamas*

Less Luggage, More Comfort

A person called Thakkar comes to test Shirdi Sai Baba. About him, Shirdi Baba says: (**Shri Sai Satcharita**, Chapter 35)

> "There was a fickle-minded gentleman. He had health and wealth and was free from both physical and mental afflictions, but he took on him needless anxieties and burdens and wandered hither and thither, thus losing his peace of mind. Sometimes he dropped the burdens and at other times carried them again. His mind knew no steadiness. Seeing his state, I took pity on him and said, 'Now please keep your faith on any one place (point) you like, why roam like this? Stick quietly to one place'"
>
> Thakkar at once came to know that, that was an exact description of himself

Ramanachala says much the same thing in ***Nān Yār?***:

> **18. Of the devotees, who is the greatest?**
> He who gives himself up to the Self that is God is the most excellent devotee. Giving one's self up to God means remaining constantly in the Self without giving room for the rise of any thoughts other than that of the Self. Whatever burdens are thrown on God, He bears them. Since the supreme power of God makes all things move, why should we, without submitting ourselves to it,

constantly worry ourselves with thoughts as to what should be done and how, and what should not be done and how not? **We know that the train carries all loads, so after getting on it why should we carry our small luggage on our head to our discomfort, instead of putting it down in the train and feeling at ease?**

https://media.radiosai.org/journals/vol_11/01JUN13/Lessons-one-can-learn-from-a-train-journey-radiosai-article-sathya-sai-baba.htm

Brahman and Maya

Brahman is my father and Maya, my mother.
As they interlocked, I got this body
~Shirdi Sai Baba, seen in Chapter 15, ***Sai Baba the Master***

In the **Shri Sai Satcharita**, normally you find advice on how to live Life

So it was quite unusual to read this high-end material in **The Life and Teachings of Sai Baba of Shirdi**: (pp. 323~324)

> NG Chandorkar: "Who is this Maya? Who created her? What is she like? You just now said that the root of the whole world is Chaitanya. Then where does Maya come in?"
>
> Baba: "I will describe to you where and how she comes. Maya is the name given to the Shakti or Power of Chaitanya, which makes Chaitanya appear in different forms. Can you separate Chaitanya from its Shakti? You cannot, just as you cannot separate jaggery from its sweetness and the sun from its brilliance. The separation comes only at the end of Maya (if merger in Brahman is separation). Maya ends when Chaitanya is realized. Chaitanya is endless. Both Chaitanya and Maya are beginningless. Maya and Chaitanya are also named

> Prakriti and Purusha, which are fully described in the Jnanesvari from which you must get your Atma Jnana
>
> "Chaitanya is a cave and he who enters into that cave never returns but becomes the cave
>
> "Maya is Karya and has wonderful qualities. I am such and such a person, you are such and such, etc.—all this is the result of Maya. All these are unreal differences. You see, if you are under Maya, (undifferentiated) Reality does not appear. Maya has two aspects: (1) The Avarana, covering up the consciousness of the soul or Atman, and (2) Vikshepa, producing illusory appearances over that covering..."

That cave bit was very interesting:

> Chaitanya is a cave and he who enters into that cave never returns but becomes the cave

echoing the "death experience" of Ramanachala

A reference to the cave is also seen in **The Power of Arunachala**:

> When a devotee enquired about his true nature, he replied, 'Arunachala-Ramana is the Supreme Self who blissfully abides as consciousness in the heart-cave of all souls beginning with Hari (Lord Vishnu)'

Maya is the shadow of Brahman, the Self; like gravity, it comes with the territory

As Brahmachaitanya Maharaj says: (in the *pravachan* for 11.FEB)

> There are many who keenly desire to devote themselves to Rama and nama, but do not actually practise it; why is this so? This is due to the obstruction of maya. How can we outwit maya and reach God? She is like His shadow; and to expect Him to come without His shadow is as good as asking Him not to come. **Maya is thus an unavoidable accompaniment to God**

The Master explains their tango in the **Gospel**: (Chapter **38. With the Devotees in Calcutta**)

> "Kali is none other than Brahman. That which is called Brahman is really Kali. She is the Primal Energy. When that Energy remains inactive, I call It Brahman, and when It creates, preserves, or destroys, I call It Sakti or Kali. What you call Brahman I call Kali
>
> "Brahman and Kali are not different. They are like fire and its power to burn: if one thinks of fire one must think of its power to burn. If one recognizes Kali one must also recognize Brahman; again, if one recognizes Brahman one must recognize Kali. Brahman and Its Power are identical. It is Brahman whom I address as Sakti or Kali"

Much earlier, in Chapter 7, He says:

> (To Prankrishna) "Brahman and Sakti are inseparable. Unless you accept Sakti, you will find the whole universe unreal — 'I', 'you', house, buildings, and family. The world stands solid because the Primordial Energy stands behind it. If there is no supporting pole, no framework can be made, and without the framework there can be no beautiful image of Durga

And a couple of pages later:

> "But the universe and its created beings, and the twenty-four cosmic principles, all exist because God exists. Nothing remains if God is eliminated. The number increases if you put many zeros after the figure one; but the zeros don't have any value if the one is not there"

The Master further says that one can see Brahman only by removing the "scum" of Maya: (Chapter 44)

> "Further, He revealed to me a huge reservoir of water covered with green scum. The wind moved a little of the scum and immediately the water became visible; but in the twinkling of an eye, scum from all sides came dancing in and again covered the water. He revealed to me that the water was like Satchidananda, and the scum like maya. On account of maya, Satchidananda is not seen. Though now and then one may get a glimpse of It, again maya covers It"

To corroborate, in ***Nān Yār?***, Ramanachala says that only one of the two (either Maya or Brahman) can be experienced:

> **4. When will the realization of the Self be gained?**
>
> When the world which is what-is-seen has been removed, there will be realization of the Self which is the seer
>
> **5. Will there not be realization of the Self even while the world is there (taken as real)?**
>
> There will not be
>
> **6. Why?**
>
> The seer and the object seen are like the rope and the snake. Just as the knowledge of the rope which is the substrate will not arise unless the false knowledge of the illusory serpent goes, so the realization of the Self which is the substrate will not be gained unless the belief that the world is real is removed
>
> **7. When will the world which is the object seen be removed?**
>
> When the mind, which is the cause of all cognitions and of all actions, becomes quiescent, the world will disappear

Which makes me seriously wonder: what exactly did Ramanachala see after Self-Realization (*manōnāsha*)? A tantalizing mystery for me

Nisargadatta Maharaj answers this in **I Am That**:

> **7. The Mind**
>
> **Q: Surely, you see the actual world as it surrounds you. You seem to behave quite normally!**
>
> M: That is how it appears to you. What in your case occupies the entire field of consciousness, is a mere speck in mine. The world lasts, but for a moment. It is your memory that makes you think that the world continues. Myself, I don't live by memory. I see the world as it is, a momentary appearance in consciousness

So that's what distinguishes the Self-realized folks: They are able to see both sides of the coin—the Formless as well as the world of Name and Form (*nāma/rūpa*)—and live in the Now simply because there isn't anything else (past or future) for Them

Your own Self-realization is the greatest service you can render the world
~Ramanachala

Is Brahman a Fractal?

There was message from **AHAM.com**:

> Ramana Maharshi: The Self is beyond duality. If there is one there will also be two. Without one there are no other numbers. The truth is neither one nor two. It is as it is

The Master says in the **Gospel**: (Chapter **33. With Various Devotees**)

> "The Vedas speak of Satchidananda Brahman. Brahman is neither one nor two; It is between one and two. It cannot be described either as existence or as non-existence; It is between existence and non-existence"

Which makes me wonder whether Brahman is a fractal, with a dimension between one and two (1.58 as per **Fractal Dimension** at http://math.bu.edu/DYSYS/chaos-game/node6.html)

It certainly does exhibit those characteristics

Prof. GV Subbaramayya reminisces in **Face to Face with Sri Ramana Maharshi**: (Section 41)

> In the evening Bhagavan referred to the description of the Self as "the smallest of atoms, the biggest of big things". He said, "The hailstone falls in the ocean. At once it melts and becomes the ocean itself. Likewise, the source of the Self is a pinpoint. When it is searched for, it disappears, and only the fullness remains"

One of the interesting things about fractals is that unless the **scale** of a fractal (image) is known, there's no way to tell what it is!

For me, the best example of a fractal is when Mother Yashoda suspects Baby Krishna to be eating mud, which He denies. When she asks Him to open His mouth to check, she ends up seeing the Universe!

Peccavi

Swami Vivekananda said:

> "The Vedanta recognizes no sin; it only recognizes error. And the greatest error, says the Vedanta is to say that you are weak, that you are a sinner, a miserable creature, and that you have no power and you cannot do this and that"

Eckhart Tolle writes in **A New Earth** that the original meaning of sin was "missing the mark"

In **Arunachala Shiva**, the second chapter starts with a quote by Ramanachala: (page 11)

> The greatest error of a man is to think that he is weak by nature, evil by nature. Every man is divine and strong in his real nature. What are weak are his habits, his desires and thoughts, but not himself

*Note: the title of this chapter is a doff to one of the greatest puns ever made, in **Punch**, Saturday 18th May 1844*

Foreign Affairs.

IT is a common idea that the most laconic military despatch ever issued was that sent by CÆSAR to the Horse-Guards at Rome, containing the three memorable words "*Veni, vidi, vici,*" and, perhaps, until our own day, no like instance of brevity has been found. The despatch of SIR CHARLES NAPIER, after the capture of Scinde, to LORD ELLENBOROUGH, both for brevity and truth, is, however, far beyond it. The despatch consisted of one emphatic word—"*Peccavi,*" "I have Scinde," (*sinned*).

https://commons.wikimedia.org/wiki/File:18440518-Peccavi_Punch.jpg

For the Love of Dad

During *Navarātri* of 2012, one of our outside taps went kaput and Venkatesh, the plumber, came to fix a new one. He was looking a bit lost generally and told me about his Dad, who went missing some time back

Looks like he had Alzheimer's and they're unable to trace his whereabouts. Venkatesh was trying to take out ads in newspapers, but they cost ₹15,000 per state, and he had to cover three of them (Karnataka, Andhra Pradesh, and Tamil Nadu). We collected some money but that was still very far from meeting his expenses

One evening, he came home and told me the important news: he found his Dad!

He was looked after by a well-to-do family, about 35 km from Tiruvannamalai (TVM), for the last 50 days. They themselves had lost one of their elders, who went missing, and one of the kids in the family saw Venkatesh's Dad at a bus station. He wasn't asking for money, but sitting at the same place and crying for two days. So they took him in, treating as a gesture from Arunachala Himself, to replace their missing elder

The funny thing was that he went missing from there as well for a week, but they found him back. Since he couldn't speak Tamil and responded with shakes of the head, the TVM family thought he was a mute

In the meanwhile, Venkatesh was doing different routes, sticking paper ads in various bus stations. TV channels don't do missing-person ads, but the Railways checked for him the length & breadth of the country and gave him a clean chit (his Dad wasn't at any of the railway stations)

Interestingly, one of the kids of the TVM family, who normally travels by car, ended up going to the bus station and seeing the missing-person ad for the person who was staying at their house. The family debated for a couple of days and felt that the proper thing to do was to call the numbers indicated in the ad. And they called all **ten** of them!

That's how Venkatesh got his Dad back. What struck me most was that the guy never gave up searching!

A Thought Experiment

Started an interesting experiment

There's a person constantly chattering away in the head, aka the mind

Is the mind you? Most possibly not

The mind is the **bed** from which all thoughts are bubbling up continuously

The system can't restrict such thoughts. It might lose a great thought with such constraints. So all thoughts bubble up, **untrammeled**

It's the job of the intelligence to do that check on thoughts: sensible or not, actionable or not, etc

Now there's a **third** guy watching the mind as well as the intelligence

That's **You**, cutting across all the states: waking, dream, and deep sleep

So my experiment is to cut the crap from the mind

Just keep watching the thought, without any allegiance to it: it's **a** thought, it's not **my** thought

via WhatsApp

For the Self-realized folks, the mind has been **annihilated**: *manōnāsha*

David Godman alludes to Sadguru being like radio boxes: they seem to be behaving like regular folks, but when you open them up, you find nothing in Them: they are just **Receivers**!

Eckhart Tolle notes: When Ramanachala was asked how to gauge one's own spiritual progress, He said by the degree of absence of thought

Papaji writes of Ramanachala:

> When I was at Ramanasramam in the 1940s I used to spend hours looking at the Maharshi's eyes. They would be open and staring, but not focused on anything. Though his eyes were open, they were not seeing anything. Those eyes were completely free of thoughts and desires. The mind is revealed very clearly in the eyes, but in those eyes there was nothing at all to see. In the hours that I concentrated on his eyes, I didn't once see even a flicker of a thought or a desire. I have not seen such utterly desire-less eyes like his on any other face. I have met many great saints during my life, but no one has impressed me as much as the Maharshi did

Playing Second Fiddle

Q: Which musical instrument is most difficult to play?

With devotees thronging the Sadguru, i am always intrigued by the sideshows along the way. How does one devotee react when another is shown, say, more grace?

It just depends on what **you** bring to the table

Ramanachala was quite nonchalant about it. He would say that He couldn't do anything if one devotee brought a cup to the ocean and another a jug

From the reminiscences of Prof. GV Subbaramayya in **Face to Face with Sri Ramana Maharshi**: (Section 41)

> One day in December 1939, Devaraja Mudaliar, an intimate devotee, asked how Bhagavan could observe distinction among His devotees. "For instance", he added, "Shall we be wrong if we say that Subbaramayya is shown a little more favor than others?" Bhagavan smilingly replied, "To me there is no distinction. Grace is flowing like the ocean ever full. Everyone draws from it according to capacity. How can one who brings only a tumbler complain that he is not able to take as much as another who brought a jar?"

via WhatsApp

Dissolving Challenges

One thing i really love about Ramanachala is how He **dissolves** challenges

From **Ramana Periya Puranam**: (page 260)

> They [Paul Brunton and Major AW Chadwick] went to Bhagavan and Chadwick asked him, "Bhagavan, is *brahmacharya*, celibacy, necessary for spiritual seekers?" **Bhagavan's method of answering was never just to solve the problem. His answers were always focused on dissolving it**. He replied, "To remain unmoved in Brahman is *brahmacharya*. The very word *brahmacharya* indicates that you should not move away from Brahman. So, staying unmoved in the 'I AM' is very essential for seekers"

I used to be afraid of public speaking and this simple but profound Q&A (opposite) with Ramanachala **dissolved** it in a jiffy

About the Author

Srinivas Shastri was born in Vizag in 1965, on the edge of Infinity, with Ramakrishna Beach separating his house on a promontory from the Bay of Bengal, the largest bay in the world

He studied Mechanical Engineering at Andhra University College of Engineering and majored in Systems and Finance at IIM, Ahmedabad in the mid~1980s

Work was a bit of a shock for him. Somehow he did about 19 years of that, before retiring in 2006 for good. The best experience was working on the Executive Search app for Maars India, where he gleaned many nuggets about the Net, such as asynchronous design

This is his third book, after:

- *Brushes with Brahmn ~ Dancing with my Datta [https://g.co/kgs/9qycik]*
- *Ma Narmada PariCarMa ~ A Pictorial Essay of a Parikrama [https://g.co/kgs/VXDaLx]*